CHAPTER ONE

THE WILDS OF PHINNEY'S RIDGE

"HERE BEAR, FOX, BIRD and all other species of wild animals will revel in luxury," reported the *Seattle Daily Press* in 1889. The paper was describing the new Woodland Park, north of town. The park was owned and operated by flamboyant local businessman Guy Carleton Phinney, and would later become the home of Seattle's Woodland Park Zoo.

But it doesn't appear that the original animals, whether native or imported, were intended to serve as exhibits. There was a hunting lodge and a deer herd acquired in California on the property, as well as imported quail—elements of the hunting culture of aristocratic English country life.

In 1891, French actress Sarah Bernhardt, appearing locally in Sardou's *Fédora*, rode across the Phinney estate to Green Lake loaded for bear. Bear tracks were spotted, but the quarry could not be found. Instead, the diva bagged a squirrel and some birds, including a

flicker and a jay. She was also said to have been entertained by the Phinneys with a lavish party.

Woodland Park was a hybrid—both a public park to promote nearby residential lots for sale in Phinney's new real estate development, and a pseudo English country estate with Phinney as its squire.

Phinney, a dapper and imposing figure standing over six feet tall and weighing about 300 pounds, had bought 364 acres north of the city in early 1889. His acreage ran across the top of the ridge north of the town of Fremont (later to become a Seattle neighborhood) and down the ridge's east side to Green Lake. Phinney paid $10,000 for the land that today is bounded by 64th Street to the north, 45th Street to the south, Green Lake Way to the east, and Phinney Avenue North to the west. The next day, he sold a small corner of the expanse for $3,500. He also sold all the giant old-growth trees—some more than six feet in diameter.

The real estate that remained included the lots for sale and what is now Lower Woodland Park,

LEFT: Guy Phinney (on far right) on a social outing in Woodland Park, circa 1890s.

ABOVE: One of Guy Phinney's private streetcars near the Woodland Park entrance, circa 1895.

BELOW: The zoo's Beech Grove predates the zoo itself.

Woodland Park Zoo, and the adjacent section of today's Aurora Avenue North, about 50 residential blocks. After his quick land and timber sales, Phinney had acquired it all for the net sum of $6,200.

Phinney began making various improvements to what he called Woodland (or sometimes, Woodlands) Park. He removed nearly all of the native conifers from the upper portion of the park, where he envisioned his English park, and planted European beeches (*Fagus sylvatica*) that still stand on the zoo's grounds.

Phinney built a gatehouse where he lived with his wife, the former Nell Wright, and their two boys while preparing to build a large stately home. Another English landed-gentry touch was the small Episcopal church that Phinney built west of the park. He also paid for its furniture, operating expenses, and the vicar's salary. On Sundays, his sons were sent ahead to ring the church bell. Guy Phinney, wearing a black frock coat and top hat, led a procession from the park to church.

The lower portion of the park was left more or less alone, with a winding road leading down through the forest to the shores of Green Lake. His landholding was referred to as Phinney's Ridge. Today, the neighborhood

The Gatehouse home of the Phinneys (left), with Guy Phinney's two young boys, Arthur and Walter, on the far right road, circa 1891. The hotel is visible to the far right.

that sits between Greenwood to the north and Fremont to the south, Ballard to the west, and Green Lake to the east is known as Phinney Ridge, and Phinney Avenue runs along the spine of the ridge. It was outside the city limits until 1891, when Phinney Ridge, Green Lake, and Fremont, along with several other neighborhoods, were annexed by the City of Seattle.

Phinney was born on May 30, 1852, in Nova Scotia, and was educated there and at Phillips Exeter Academy in New Hampshire. He was accepted at Harvard but went to a university in Quebec instead, where he studied mathematics. Clearly of an adventurous bent, he dropped out of law school at Montreal's McGill

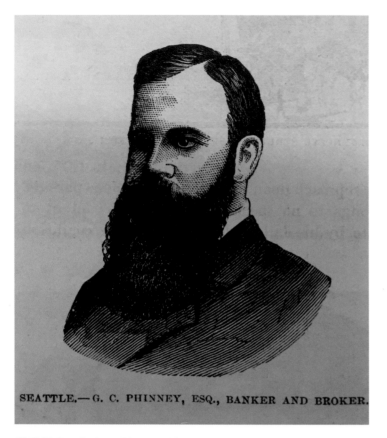

SEATTLE.—G. C. PHINNEY, ESQ., BANKER AND BROKER.

ABOVE: Guy Carleton Phinney, 1886.

Phinney for general law, collection and insurance business. After the lapse of a year he bought out the interest of his partner and carried on the business by himself. All the profits of his business were invested in real estate and today, in addition to his hold-ings in the Phinney, Carleton and Butler blocks (the latter cost $180,000), he owns Woodland Park, in which he has invested large sums of money in improvements and has converted it into a veritable paradise. He is building a residence at Woodland Park at a cost of $80,000. Mr. Phinney's only business now is banking; he is a most genial man, and of fine presence.

BELOW: Guy Phinney's personal electric trolley soon began to carry passengers from Fremont up to the park.

University to try his hand at the mining business in British Columbia. After some success, he went broke and then made his way to San Francisco, where he spent a few months before working his passage north to Seattle in February 1881 on the steamship *Olympus*.

The *Olympus* caught fire about 600 miles off the mouth of the Columbia River. That evening Phinney and 25 others in a lifeboat were picked up by a ship that landed at Point Discovery. From there Phinney made his way to Seattle to make his fortune.

An 1890 article in *Seattle Illustrated* described Guy Phinney's rise to success:

For a short period, he filled a position as clerk, but shortly afterward formed the firm of Nelson &

Green house
Woodland P...
S...

One of the many features Guy Phinney added to his property was this greenhouse.

In 1889, electric streetcars came to Seattle, relieving horses of the burden of hauling streetcars up Seattle's steep slopes. This was the first appearance of electric streetcars on the West Coast, and Seattleites were awestruck. In *History of King County*, Clarence Bagley described the first day of operation:

There was no ceremony, but the excitement was tremendous . . . all Seattle lined Second Avenue to watch the cars go by. Every time a car stopped the curiosity of the people nearly disrupted the service, as it was with difficulty that the most venturesome were restrained from crawling under the car to see what made it go.

By the end of 1890, Phinney had his own short line bringing potential customers to his real estate development. Passengers could transfer from the Seattle Consolidated Street Railway to Phinney's line down the hill from Woodland Park in Fremont. He had a second streetcar for his personal use, allowing him to commute downtown in comparative comfort. It was painted white and nicknamed The White Elephant.

Stranded Sami Camp Out

· · · · · · ·

In 1898, widow Nell Phinney allowed hundreds of reindeer and their herders to stay at Woodland Park when they were stranded in Seattle.

The indigenous people of northern Europe who herd, milk, and train reindeer for pulling sleds called pulkas were then called Laplanders, but today they are known as the Sami. The Sami and their reindeer were on an aid mission to snowbound miners in Alaska who were in danger of starving. The U.S. Congress had allocated funds to hire Sami herders and their harness-trained reindeer to deliver sleds of supplies.

The Sami and their stock had sailed from Bosekop, Norway, to New York. The expedition included 113 Sami men, women, and children; 539 reindeer; 418 sleds; several herd dogs; and a supply of lichen to feed the reindeer.

They arrived in New York on February 28, after a 26-day journey. From New York they traveled by train to Seattle, arriving on March 7, only to discover that the expedition might be canceled because the miners were no longer starving, and that the ship that was supposed to take them to Alaska had departed instead for the Philippines to pick up Spanish-American War troops.

During a long delay in Seattle, a five-year-old Sami boy died, the lichen supply was mistaken for packing material and thrown away, and their reindeer were set out to pasture

Reindeer on their way to Alaska from Norway were put out to pasture in Woodland Park, but the lawn was no substitute for their native lichen.

Men and horses of the Third U.S. Cavalry camped near Green Lake en route to the Philippines in 1899.

at Woodland Park—a bad idea because the lawn was the wrong food for them. A Sami interpreter was located in the Scandinavian neighborhood of Ballard, and Sami families camped and tended their reindeer at Woodland Park for two weeks. They quickly became the focal point of local curiosity, and an estimated 10,000 people came out to see them. While in Seattle, 12 reindeer died either from starvation or from inappropriate food.

The women and children traveled to Fort Townsend (now Fort Townsend State Park), Washington, while 57 Sami men and 527 starving reindeer were shipped to Haines, Alaska, under sail aboard the *Seminole*. Most of the reindeer died and most of the men returned to Fort Townsend to rejoin their families and friends. Eventually, the remaining Sami traveled to Alaska on two separate ships, establishing reindeer stations that helped build herds to provide food, clothing, and transportation during the Gold Rush and into the 1920s and '30s. For a time, reindeer were even used to carry mail.

Several of the families settled in Poulsbo, Washington, on Puget Sound, after completing their work in Alaska, and their descendants held a reunion there in 1998. Many of the single Sami men married Inuit women, and their descendants live in Alaska.

The Sami and their reindeer were not the only unanticipated campers at Woodland Park needing help from Nell Phinney. In August of 1899, after the United States had defeated Spain in the Spanish-American War, members of the Third U.S. Cavalry camped at lower Green Lake while their horses were stationed in Woodland Park. The men and their horses were waiting to sail across the Pacific to put down the insurrection by Filipinos who had fought with the United States against Spain, but now wanted to prevent American control of the recently conquered Philippine Islands.

For Heaven's Sake, Don't Bring Your Dog!

· · · · · · · ·

Alongside the stone archway near the main entry at 50th Street and Fremont Avenue North was a large sign with Guy Phinney's park rules. Plants and wildlife were not to be disturbed. Guns, alcohol, gambling, and cursing were prohibited, and no dogs were allowed. In fact, they would be shot on sight.

Read these Rules and Regulations before entering
WOODLAND PARK.

1. This is a Private Park, but free to all persons who obey these rules, and conduct themselves in an orderly manner.

2. Positively no dogs allowed in this Park. Any dog seen within its limits will be shot.

3. Any person carrying a gun or discharging firearms within the Park limits will be arrested and fined to the fullest extent of the law.

4. Any person picking Flowers, Wild flowers, Moss & or cutting or marring any Tree, Shrub or Plant and or building within the Park limits will be arrested and dealt with according to law.

5. All persons will please turn off the water after using it.

6. Any person driving on the walks where driving is prohibited by notice will be arrested and fined.

7. Any person molesting or teasing any bird or animal or disturbing any bird's nest will be arrested and fined.

8. All profane, vulgar and improper language of any kind is strictly prohibited.

9. No games will be offered in Woodland Park on Sunday till after 12 O clock noon.

10. Gambling of any and all kinds within the Park limits is strictly prohibited.

— G. C. PHINNEY

In 1892, Phinney got the City Council to designate two of his employees—William Grass and J. Edward Bladine—and himself as "special park police" to enforce the law and his posted rules. Each of the three was paid one dollar a year.

Pathways and landscaping on the estate changed a dense Northwest forest into an open English garden. Phinney added a hotel, a greenhouse, and a ball field. The hunter's pavilion and a small boathouse were built along the lakeshore. Phinney also built a glass conservatory near what was later to become the zoo's South Entrance.

By 1893 it seemed that things couldn't have been going better for Guy Phinney. But just before he was about to build his mansion, he died at the age of 42. Phinney left his estate to his two boys when they became 21, with his wife as executrix. He also left instructions that his properties could be sold as needed to settle probate, but "always reserving until the last necessity Woodland Park." (Will of Guy Carleton Phinney)

With the Panic of 1893, the worst financial decline in U.S. history to that time, the real-estate sales that had provided the estate's income came to a complete halt. Nell Phinney got permission from the City Council to discontinue streetcar service down the hill to Fremont. There weren't enough riders to pay for its operation. With the economy finally moving again in 1897 and 1898, she was able to sell the line and cars to the Seattle Tractor Company. The Phinney Streetcar Line eventually became the #5 Metro bus line, which follows much of the same route. Gentle S-turns along sections of this route exist where tracks once carried streetcars around its curves and more than a century later work well for long, articulated buses.

Not long after the sale of the streetcar line, Nell offered to sell the privately owned park of nearly 200 acres to the City of Seattle for $140,972. Many felt that it cost too much and was too far out of town, but overriding a veto by Mayor Thomas J. Humes, the City Council approved the purchase in late 1899.

A stone archway marked the entrance to the park.

Litigation associated with some of Phinney's business activities and infighting over the estate among relatives went on for years. From 1894 to 1906, Nell Phinney was listed as the defendant in 36 civil cases in King County Court. Nell Phinney, no doubt exhausted from settling the estate, moved with her children to Victoria, British Columbia, where Phinneys, including Guy Carleton Phinney IV, were still living more than a century later.

CHAPTER TWO

MENAGERIES MERGE, ANIMALS ARRIVE, BUILDING BEGINS

SHORTLY BEFORE HIS DEATH, Guy Phinney had added some ostriches to his wildlife collection, but the menagerie at Woodland Park began to shrink during the late 1890s. By 1899, a newspaper article refers to only four deer being housed in the park. That was soon to change.

Across the city on the shores of Lake Washington in the Leschi neighborhood, there was another park. People reached it by cable car to swim and picnic, enjoy the vaudeville theater and casino, and take paddle-wheel lake tours. Two trained sea lions in an aquatic pen performed for visitors seated in a grandstand. A small menagerie included, at various times, monkeys, a puma, elk, bears, and goats.

In 1903, the company that owned the menagerie and the railway gave the remaining animals to the City to be transferred to Woodland Park. The sea lions didn't come, because there wasn't a facility for them at Woodland Park, but the Park Board's 1904 annual

report said that "three elk, three pea fowls and three bears" from Leschi were moved to Woodland Park. Other animals had already begun to accumulate there. Several eagles arrived at the zoo between 1900 and 1902, possibly from a small menagerie at Volunteer Park consisting of "five deer, two eagles, one owl and one fox." (*Seattle Post-Intelligencer*, 1901)

By April 1904, a *Seattle Post-Intelligencer* article reported, "Going to see the animals is a familiar phrase to street car men, as half the population of Seattle has flocked to Woodland since it has been known as a zoological park." The collection was skimpy, and some of the exhibits might even have been considered local nuisance animals, but it grew through breeding and donations.

In 1904, citizens of Seward, Alaska, gave the zoo a brown bear named Carrie Nation after the hatchet-wielding temperance crusader who busted up saloons. The first animal inventory for Woodland Park Zoo was written the same year. There were eight species of mammals and nine species of birds. The list included

LEFT: The polar bear exhibit (right) and umbrella pool for seals (left), circa 1924.

19 deer, five elk, two brown bears, eight black bears, two coyotes, one raccoon, one coatimundi, four guinea pigs, six peafowl, six eagles, three owls, one swan, one Muscovy duck, one pheasant, four ring doves, three brant (a wild goose species), and three gulls.

Many zoos of the era had beginnings even less auspicious than Woodland Park's. They were dumping grounds for unwanted exotic pets, animals from local hunters or world travelers, and stranded animals from bankrupt circuses and other traveling shows. The press and much of the general public referred to the zoo at

An early bear pit exhibit, circa 1908.

Woodland Park as a "menagerie." At the time, most zoos fit today's definition of a menagerie—miscellaneous collections of displaced or donated animals, displayed with little or no thematic organization.

Menageries had been assembled since antiquity, often as symbols of wealth and prestige. Some private menageries in Europe were eventually opened to the public. Americans viewed them as cultural institutions that should be emulated. By the early 1900s, there was a steady increase in the number of menageries in large American cities. Establishing a zoo became a matter of civic pride.

Guy Phinney had encouraged visitors to bring picnic lunches to Woodland Park, but by 1904 visitors could also buy lunches, peanuts, and candy from a concessionaire. About a third of the peanuts were fed to zoo animals by visitors. A 1906 report said the animals had become "persistent beggars."

Animals were housed in rustic lean-tos and sheds in fenced areas, and the animals had to be cold tolerant, as there was no heating capability. Some structures for animals reflected a concern for their well-being and specific needs. An eagle cage was big enough to allow flight, and its structures provided shade, shelter, and different perching locations, but there was no effort to represent the birds' natural habitat. It was dramatically different from the zoo's 21st-century eagle exhibit, with its simulated nest of real twigs, upright snags, running water, and live trees.

In 1899, Seattle's "pound master," Walter Washington, whose main job was dealing with stray cows, horses, and other domestic animals that occasionally wandered through the city, was given responsibility for the care of the animals in Woodland Park. But by 1902, John P. Reynolds, a Pennsylvania native born in 1855, was listed in the city directory as "assistant park keeper" for Woodland Park. In 1906, he was given

The zoo's eagle flight cage, circa 1915.

the newly created post of "animal keeper," at $65 per month. In 1907, Reynolds moved onto the grounds of Woodland Park, and, in 1908, he was promoted to "park keeper" and his salary was raised to $80 a month.

Reynolds left Woodland Park not long after this promotion to take on the job of creating the grounds and pathways of the city's Alaska-Yukon-Pacific Exposition. Many years later, in November 1933, then zoo director Dr. Gus Knudson welcomed the 77-year-old Reynolds to the zoo. Knudson wrote:

Mr. Reynolds, a former director of the zoo, was a visitor. At the time he was in charge of the zoo there were only a few specimens. Of course he is interested in the upbuilding of the institution and watches the advancements made. Mr. Reynolds asked especially to see Carrie Nation, the large Alaskan Brown Bear which was only a young thing when he was director. He couldn't help but marvel at the changes which have been made since he was in charge of the zoo and is trying in his own way to bring the zoo to the top.

In the summer of 1903, the City Council hired the Olmsted Brothers of Brookline, Massachusetts, the nation's first landscape architecture firm. It had been founded by Frederick Law Olmsted, the designer of New York's Central Park and the University of California, Berkeley, and Stanford University campuses. The Council asked for a comprehensive plan for Seattle's parks. The Olmsteds' report was accepted and approved by the Council on October 19, 1903.

John Charles Olmsted (1852-1920), the stepson of Frederick Law Olmsted, was the firm's principal designer in Seattle. His 1903 master plan laid out a 20-mile-long system of parks and playfields along scenic boulevards, lowered and landscaped Green Lake, and redesigned Woodland Park on Guy Phinney's former estate. The plan for Woodland Park included both rectilinear grids and curvilinear trails and parkways that followed the topography of the land. The Olmsteds had specific recommendations for the zoo:

The lower portion of the park is too beautiful and the limited area will be too much needed for the accommodation of crowds of visitors to justify the sacrifice of any part of it to the purposes of a menagerie. There should be no enclosures for deer or elk or other pasturing animals in the lower part of the park. There being less natural beauty in the upper portion of the park, since it is flat and has no view, and has been mainly cleared of the original forest, it would be comparatively unobjectionable, if it be thought desirable, to devote part of this portion of the park largely to a collection of hardy wild animals.
(Olmsted Report, 1903)

Seattle voters approved three bond issues, providing the Park Board with funds to implement the Olmsted Plan: $500,000 (1906); $1 million (1908); and $2 million (1910). These were hefty allocations at the time. The total budget for maintaining all of Woodland Park in 1904, including the care of animals, was just $6,000.

In 1907, 26-year-old veterinarian Gus Knudson was hired as animal keeper. Knudson, the youngest of 10 children, had run away from his Minnesota farm at the age of 10 to join the Lemon Brothers' Circus. He traveled with the circus for several years, learning to care for exotic animal species, and he followed a course of study offered by the Veterinary Science Association.

Woodland Park, circa 1904.

Dr. Gus Knudson.

Knudson was considered a fun-loving guy. He would obligingly mug for local newspapers, which often ran light-hearted features about the zoo and its animals. On Groundhog Day in the 1930s, Knudson filled in as groundhog (since the zoo lacked one) and was photographed looking for his shadow. But he shrewdly used the publicity he got from kidding around with the press to get across his serious concerns about the zoo, including the cruelty of visitors feeding dangerous objects to the animals and the need for more budget to care for the animals properly.

An old postcard in his photo album shows a crude wooden shack at the back of the deer yard. Written

BELOW: The zoo's first director, Gus Knudson, used the shed at the back of the deer exhibit for office space.

THE DEER IN WOODLAND PARK, SEATTLE

sarcastically in block letters is "Office of the New Zoo Director, 1908," with an arrow pointing to the shack. He didn't become the zoo's first official director until 1922, but there was no question that he had been in charge since his arrival.

By 1908, the zoo was home to elk, reindeer, wolves, foxes, monkeys, seals, and buffalo, or bison. The addition of buffalo to the collection was significant because the species was then at the brink of extinction. In 1922, the herd of six all died suddenly. Knudson wrote, "Post mortem examinations were made by competent authorities, who found no trace of poison or disease, and the cause of death still remains a mystery."

Bears had been a part of the original Phinney collection, and they were kept in pits. The first barred

ABOVE: A zoo visitor communes with a brown bear housed in an enclosure built in 1908.

enclosures for bears were built in 1908 from concrete and steel. They included trellis-like ornamentation, a style that had been the standard in larger zoos since at least the 1840s. The holding areas below the exhibit floor, however, were notoriously difficult to clean and maintain.

Nickel and Dime Rides

· · · · · · ·

Animal rides were typical of the zoo's focus on children in its early years.
In 1905, a concessionaire sold burro rides, and in 1914, the zoo built its first pony ring. Both rides cost a nickel.

The zoo's first pony ring was built in 1914. Although the ring had to be rebuilt several times, pony rides were offered for the next 93 years.

In 1920, the *Seattle Post-Intelligencer* (*P-I*) proposed a fund-raising drive to buy an elephant for the zoo. Actually, the newspaper had already bought the elephant from a vaudeville act called Singer's Midgets, counting on the public to reimburse them for most of the cost through a children's penny drive and other donations.

In June 1921, the newspaper presented the female Asian elephant to the zoo after a celebratory parade through downtown Seattle. Although she was billed as a "midget" elephant during her vaudeville years, she was small only because of her age. She came to the zoo when she was about eight years old. Her show name was Cleopatra, but she was renamed in honor of the Wide Awake Club, a *P-I* children's group.

For 10 cents, a child could go for a ride on Wide Awake's back, but the rides came to an end after Wide Awake headed down a public street outside the unfenced zoo's boundary. Wide Awake remained a celebrity at the zoo until 1967, when she died at the age of 54.

Wide Awake got her own barn the year after her arrival, in 1922. A camel house was built south of the elephant house, and the zoo offered camel rides for a dime. The camels Nile and Potentate were donated by Seattle Shriners—members of the Ancient Arabic Order of the Nobles of the Mystic Shrine—a fraternity of fez-wearing Masons.

Wide Awake giving a ride.

The Primate House, originally named the Simianary, was completed in 1911. It was surrounded by well-manicured lawns and plantings like those found around museums and libraries, and on university campuses. It featured the symmetry and elegant detail typical of many American zoo buildings of the time. The Primate House was home to monkeys, birds, fish, and any other animals that needed heating, and also included Knudson's office, a big step up from the shed.

The Simianary, more commonly known as the Primate House, was completed in 1911.

In the early 1900s, exhibits at Woodland Park Zoo weren't all as ornate as the Primate House or bear enclosures. Seals at this time were housed in a small concrete-ringed pool. In 1913, an umbrella-shaped form was placed over the top of the pool, providing shade and overhead shelter for the seals.

By 1915, a barred polar bear exhibit was built at the north end of the row of bear enclosures, at a cost of $2,174. For the first time, naturalistic rockwork was included to relieve the flat surfaces of poured concrete. That same year, a 60-foot tapeworm was removed from a polar bear named Hannah, and preserved in a jar that according to legend is still somewhere on zoo grounds but has been misplaced. The tapeworm was named Stanley after a favorite measuring device.

Other additions in 1915 were an exhibit for three Asiatic leopards and a kangaroo house. A modest leopard house and a new bison corral were built in 1917 and 1918. Springbok barns and the Pheasantry, later called the Conservation Aviary, were built in 1925.

The umbrella pool, under snow, with bear cages at left and Primate House (Simianary) at right. The 1913 umbrella pool housed seals, otters, and waterfowl at different times during its history.

There was no budget to buy animals, so donations of animals were seldom refused, and the zoo would scramble to house them in quickly built temporary facilities that became more or less permanent, or in existing retrofitted buildings.

Fraternal organizations liked to donate their trademark animals. The Loyal Order of Moose donated a moose, the Benevolent and Protective Order of Elks donated elk, the Fraternal Order of Eagles donated eagles, and the Lions Club helped to acquire lions.

Animals were sometimes named after their donors. Mayor Ole Hanson gave the zoo a two-year-old lion in 1918, and a lion house was built the following year.

Ole the lion lived at the zoo until his death in 1935. Donating animals to the zoo gave people a sense of ownership and pride in the community, and zoo animals were viewed as public pets.

In 1922, Gus Knudson wrote:

From early morning until late at night visitors may be seen at the Zoo. Some come to see all of the animals; others to view special exhibits, but the most persistent visitors are the ones who take a special interest in some special pet. Very often it is one that the visitor himself has given to the Zoo, but this is not always the case. One man takes delight in the polar bear; another in a kangaroo; another in the camels.

A polar bear exhibit was built in 1915.

POLAR BEAR CAGE WOODLAND PARK
SEATTLE U.S.A.

The New Sheriff Takes On Rowdy Kids

• • • • • • •

The zoo had become an exciting destination for children and their families, but there was no admission charge and children would often come to the zoo on their own. Sometimes they teased the animals, fed them inappropriate food, and threw things into cages and corrals. Rules were posted, but there was no security staff, and enforcement was haphazard.

In 1921, 15-year-old Joseph Hahn, who loved animals and lived near the zoo, approached Gus Knudson. Joseph had seen boys poking an umbrella at Wide Awake the elephant and even throwing fish hooks into exhibits. He'd also seen other children

PROTECTOR OF THE ZOO

Joseph Hahn, Woodland Park's "zoo pony sheriff," who is the friend of all animals and is himself the "bete noir" of many a per-tiferous youngster.

climbing the rails of the camel enclosure and tugging on the hair of a baby camel.

Joseph offered to serve as a protector of the animals while he was not in school. Realizing that he would need official status to be effective, Gus Knudson was quick to appoint him "park sheriff."

Knudson issued him a cap, a sheriff's star, some handcuffs, and a billy club, which he reportedly used as he patrolled the grounds on Saturdays and holidays from 10 a.m. until 5 p.m. When Joseph was on duty, children even refrained from riding their bicycles on lawns and walkways, a rule that was typically broken.

Fifteen-year-old Joseph Hahn was made park sheriff in 1921.

One man takes great pride in a lonely old black crow. (1922 Annual Report to Seattle's Board of Park Commissioners)

Knudson understood the affection that humans felt for the animals, but he also had a more sophisticated concept of a zoo and what it should be. In 1922, he wrote what today is called a mission statement that included five goals:

To exhibit animals under favorable conditions; to foster and encourage zoological research; to increase public interest and public knowledge in wild animals and birds; to secure better protection of animal life by educational methods; to attract people from out of town to visit Seattle. (1922 Annual Report to Seattle's Board of Park Commissioners)

This 1924 view from the roof of the Primate House shows the Ferris wheel across Phinney Avenue from the zoo, built in 1919.

CHAPTER THREE

TRAFFIC, TOUGH TIMES, AND TUSKO

BY THE FAST-PACED 1920s, automobiles had changed the peaceful, sylvan landscape with which the Olmsteds had graced the city. Public roads crossed the zoo, allowing cars to shortcut from North 59th Street to Fremont Avenue North, driving past the row of bear cages. In 1911, the speed limit for cars and motorcycles at the zoo was set at 12 miles per hour on straightaways and six miles per hour on curves.

By 1927, with many more citizens now behind the wheel, an estimated 3,300 cars per day used the shortcut. The zoo and the Humane Society wanted to close the zoo's north entrance to motorized vehicles, but the neighbors and nearby businesses objected. Cars and trucks continued to rumble through the zoo for many years to come.

New roads were proposed to accommodate all the new traffic, including Highway 99, a six-lane, north-south highway through the city on Aurora Avenue. It was slated to cut right through Woodland Park.

LEFT: Tusko and G.W. "Slim" Lewis, 1932.

On June 30, 1930, by a vote of six to two, the Seattle City Council approved an ordinance extending Aurora Avenue through Woodland Park.

Councilman George Hill, who had earlier taken City Engineer R. H. Thomson on a tour of Europe to "cure him of the habit of putting roads through parks," formed a coalition to defeat the highway plan

BELOW: The zoo served as a popular shortcut for automobiles for many years, as captured in this 1915 postcard.

and proposed an alternate route following the contours of the land. Seattle's Board of Park Commissioners, the *Seattle Times,* and others joined Councilman Hill in expressing their opposition to the new highway.

Nevertheless, voters in the November election approved the ordinance, and two years later the highway sliced Woodland Park roughly in half and the zoo lost access to land that might have been used for future expansion. The two halves became known as Lower Woodland and Woodland Park Zoo.

While the new highway confined the zoo to its current acreage, the zoo's collection kept growing. By 1932, the zoo had 326 animals representing 56 species. Yet there were still only 13 employees: four animal keepers, one bird keeper, one hoofed-stock keeper, one primate keeper, two apprentices, and four laborers.

The new highway effectively split Woodland Park Zoo and Lower Woodland.

They were responsible for the animals, the buildings and grounds, and the crowds. (1932 Annual Report to Seattle's Board of Park Commissioners)

After 1929, when the Great Depression plunged the country into hard times, the zoo was also hit hard. Sometimes the zoo staff was not paid for long periods, and scrip—a substitute for currency that could be redeemed at stores in the neighborhood—was issued in lieu of pay.

Early in the Depression the zoo was almost closed to save money. Irate employee Ed Johnson, later to become zoo director, sat down on February 1, 1933, and drafted a letter to the Board of Park Commissioners that began, "Gentlemen: I have read with dissatisfaction in the newspapers of your intentions to abolish our city zoo . . . To deprive men women & children of their only source of amusement and education in the present times is not only unjust but poor sense." He suggested that if they went ahead with this plan, "your poor judgment becomes more highly emphasized." He pointed out that they had spent thousands of dollars of zoo revenue that had been handed over to the city to build a horseshoe court for "privileged citizens," and a bowling green enjoyed by just eight "privileged people." It is doubtful that the letter, drafted in pencil, was ever sent, but Johnson established that he cherished the egalitarian and democratic nature of the zoo, and understood the role it would play during hard times.

That same year, the City of Spokane was also having financial difficulties and offered to give all its zoo animals to Seattle. The City of Seattle declined. In fact, the Park Board moved that "superfluous and uninteresting animals" at Woodland Park Zoo be disposed of. They didn't say exactly what kinds of animals were considered surplus.

To feed herbivores, zoo staff had already been driving around from one grocer to another to pick up donated

The Model Farm and a New Look

· · · · · · ·

Up until the 1930s, the zoo's animal exhibits were organized taxonomically. Visitors would go to one area to see the reptiles, another to see birds, another to see bears. The first alternative to this approach was the zoo's model farm, built in 1933. There was a growing realization that urban children had become disconnected from the origin of the foods and materials they used in their daily lives. Gus Knudson described the purpose of the model farm and its innovative look to the Park Commissioners:

The most outstanding accomplishment at the zoo in 1933 was the construction of a model farm, which covers about five acres. The building is of cedar log construction, the fences and corrals being of the homemade split rail type. We believe that this feature will be of beneficial interest, especially to children who have not had the pleasure of visiting a real farm. Domestic animals will be transferred to this location as soon as the farm is completed. Adjoining this area we built a pony shelter of cedar logs, which harmonizes with the farm construction, and the appearance of which seems very appropriate for this portion of the park. (Annual Report to Seattle's Board of Park Commissioners, 1936)

The model farm was a significant undertaking for the period, and it looked a lot different from the more formal architecture of the Primate House, Elephant House, and bear exhibits, which were surrounded by manicured flower beds and lawns. The rustic model farm was also built against a backdrop of mostly native vegetation. It was a radical departure that foreshadowed Woodland Park Zoo's design philosophy of 40 years later.

This was no accident. Gus Knudson was a proponent of using native species in zoo landscaping. In a press interview he complained about the removal of native evergreens and the use of imported species, and was quoted as saying, "This is the Evergreen State, and it is fitting that in this park at least, we should preserve our own evergreen trees." He also complained about non-native holly and its sharp leaves that were inhospitable to wild birds.

The model farm, shown here in 1934, represented a break with the formal architecture of existing buildings.

produce, bread, and other food. The Depression made these donations even more important. They were augmented by fruits and vegetables grown at the City's own Carkeek Park, as well as fresh "hay" in the form of lawn clippings from other parks and parkways.

Historically, food for carnivores had consisted of donated animals, including horses, goats, cows, and sheep from the Animal Pound and Humane Society. Horses that were too old to work or had broken legs were donated by individuals. Zookeepers slaughtered many of these animals on-site.

The zoo revenues from animal rides and from refreshment and novelty concessionaires went back to the City. The zoo also sold the hides of some of

During the Great Depression there were few resources and a lot of hungry mouths to feed.

the animals slaughtered for food or that died on the grounds.

One unexpected expense during the Depression was to house and feed Tusko, the largest elephant in captivity. Tusko, a male, had been captured at the age of six in Thailand, then known as Siam. He was only about five feet tall when he stepped off a sailing ship in New York in 1898.

By 1922, he had reached a height of 10 feet, 2 inches and was advertised as "the largest elephant ever in captivity." Even though he was seven inches shorter than Phineas T. Barnum's Jumbo of the 1880s, he was at least a ton heavier. Tusko's career as a performing animal included defeating six bulls in a Juárez, Mexico, arena.

Tusko's eventful May 15, 1922, escape in Sedro-Woolley, Washington, north of Seattle, became national news. The Al G. Barnes Circus had come to town and set up its tents. When Tusko's leg irons were removed so he could be cleaned half an hour before show time, he broke away from his handler and fled. Immediately, circus personnel mounted two other elephants and began to pursue him through the streets of town.

Tusko headed north, allegedly mowing down trees, tipping over a telephone pole, ripping up fences, and bashing a Model T. He nearly burst through the back door of a speakeasy, broke into a barn where he ate some hay, and destroyed a chicken coop.

Tusko peered through the living room window of a family on Township Street and pushed on the glass. He was driven off by men throwing a woodpile at him. A local doctor, who went outside in his pajamas to see what was going on, was startled and leapt into some rosebushes when Tusko's huge face loomed up at him in the dark.

At 9:00 a.m. the next day, he was cornered against some boxcars in a gravel pit. Tusko's run for freedom cost Al Barnes $20,000 in damages. Tusko was later sold to an amusement park in Portland, Oregon, where he destroyed several pavilions after being spooked by a low-flying stunt plane. He became the center of so much trouble that he was dubbed "The Great Unwanted." In the fall of 1932, he was in Seattle, being displayed in chains on a flatbed truck at the corner

This advertisement for a traveling circus featured Tusko and Al G. Barnes.

In 1932, Tusko arrived at the zoo after a career in show business and a sad history of neglect.

of Westlake and Virginia Street by his latest owner, H. C. Barber.

Mayor John F. Dore saw Tusko there and was appalled by his condition. He ordered him confiscated and taken to the zoo, where he arrived on October 8. Children subscribed to a special fund to pay for his feed, and donations were solicited for his overall care. Wide Awake's Elephant House was enlarged to make room for Tusko, and an elephant trainer,

George Washington "Slim" Lewis, was hired to tend to the animal at $3.25 a day.

Tusko, well treated and docile at long last, died on June 10, 1933, from a massive blood clot in his heart. Although housed at the zoo, Tusko remained technically the property of his last owner, H. C. Barber, from whom he had been rescued. Barber promptly sued the city, claiming $25,000 for "lost income" due to Tusko's demise.

Mayor Dore implied that Barber's negligence was the real cause of Tusko's death. Meanwhile, Barber had Tusko rendered, with the idea of displaying both his mounted skeleton and his stuffed hide, complete with chains and shackles. University of Washington students helped dissect Tusko, and his bones went on the road as a sideshow attraction. In the 1950s, Barber's son donated Tusko's bones to the University of Oregon's Museum of Natural History.

The Great Depression practically brought new construction and improvements to a halt until the Works Progress Administration (WPA) came to the rescue. WPA was the New Deal program that used federal money to hire the unemployed for public projects. WPA workers built a beaver pond in 1936, and three years later they created an area known as Goat Hill. More than 20 maintenance and improvement projects were completed with WPA labor in 1939. In 1940, the WPA also helped to build a barn for ponies and a popular new exhibit known as Monkey Island.

Monkey Island was made up of large rocks laid in cement and topped with two artificial trees and one real one. The 70-by-90-foot island was surrounded by a shallow moat 20 feet wide and filled with water. The monkeys could easily swim in the moat, but a wall at its far end kept them from escaping.

Monkey Island was built with help from the WPA in 1940. A keeper "skims" the pool.

Having a Heart in Hard Times

· · · · · · ·

The same year that Tusko arrived at the zoo, an old horse named Denver was donated as food for carnivores. Denver had retired from the Seattle Police Department and worked at Camp Denny, a campsite for Seattle children on the east side of Lake Washington. After Denver spent a few years giving rides to thousands of youthful campers, veterinarians recommended that the horse be put down.

Denver was city property, destined to serve as carnivore food at the zoo. However, a married couple asked if they could buy the horse and care for him. The husband had worked at Camp Denny and grown fond of Denver. Seattle's Board of Park Commissioners gave Denver to the couple without asking for any money.

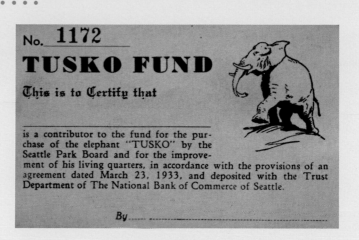

A 1933 receipt for the Tusko fund drive.

The citizens, the city, and the zoo rallied to protect vulnerable animals like Tusko and Denver, even in hard times. The zoo was seen as a collective civic responsibility, and during the Depression, it was also a place for free recreation. In subsequent years, the culture of civic ownership of the zoo fueled enthusiasm for public drives to fund the acquisition of new animals.

During the Great Depression, donations were solicited for the care of Tusko, a confiscated elephant brought to Woodland Park Zoo.

About 17 male monkeys, who had been living alone in barred cages, were placed on the island. At first, they were confused and huddled together in small groups. Not used to being in direct sunlight, they jumped when they saw their shadows.

Before long, however, they began fighting for the alpha monkey position. Local papers covered the struggles, describing them in human terms. Coco lasted maybe a day before being dethroned by a monkey named Sing, who got off to a good start by knocking

half a dozen challengers into the moat. But perhaps because of the stress of being top monkey, he was soon biting his own tail. The press reported that the other monkeys took notice and began showing signs of rebellion.

Gus Knudson, always ready to provide copy to the local press, dismissed a rumor that he intended to turn a couple of baboons loose on the island, perhaps to police the place: "They'd eat those smaller monkeys like corn on the cob," he said.

Sing's downfall was witnessed by an enthusiastic human crowd. The *Post-Intelligencer* described it as a great "naval engagement" in which Coco and Sing violently fought it out in the moat. The *Times* wrote, "When the crisis came and Sing's government fell, it was difficult to determine whether the band of monkeys on the island, or the crowd watching the revolution from the wall, was the more agitated. The crowd cheered, a woman screamed, [and] someone threw a plank into the water for Sing to escape across."

Newspaper coverage continued, and people came in droves. An estimated 25,000 persons visited the island on Sunday, August 18, 1940, and streetcars serving the zoo made 16 extra trips to handle the traffic. Eventually, the monkeys settled down and the crowds fell off.

Monkeys have both what zoos call high attraction—the ability of a species to attract visitors—and high holding power, a term that describes how much time visitors spend at an exhibit. Humans typically compare other primates with their own species, and see

Monkey Island included a schoolhouse with a bell that the monkeys could ring.

Entertaining Animals

· · · · · · ·

Through the years, certain animals, such as the elephants Wide Awake and Tusko, became celebrities at the zoo. Another crowd pleaser was Red, "the high diving Bengal monkey." The animal, weighing about 20 pounds, was trained to climb to the top of a 50-foot pole and jump into a canvas net. In 1935, Gus Knudson proudly reported to Park Commissioners, "To the best of our knowledge this is the greatest diving height of any monkey in captivity in the world at this time."

Knudson wrote, "As it is the natural instinct of this species of monkey to climb trees in their native land, leaping

Lion cubs in the window of the fashionable Frederick & Nelson store entrance entertain a crowd of children.

to the ground from the tree tops, it has not been difficult to train 'Red' for this act." He reported that "throngs" of visitors were enjoying the performances. Red was supposed to perform this feat for Vice President John Nance Garner when he visited the zoo, but according to retired keeper Gene Chriest, Red refused.

In 1935, the camel Potentate, who had been donated by local Shriners, made a visit to a Shriners convention in Tacoma. Accompanied by a zookeeper, Potentate rode to Tacoma in the zoo's trailer and was paraded on the streets in a new robe and bridle provided by the Shriners.

Potentate later ended up in the lobby of the Tacoma Hotel at the front desk, ostensibly to check in, and Knudson reported that "this caused much excitement and hilarity," adding that "[Potentate] then proceeded to the main banquet room, winding in and out around the tables amid tremendous excitement, comment and gesticulations."

The next day, after spending the night in a fire station, Potentate was featured in another parade and various initiation ceremonies, amusing the partying Shriners until past midnight. Using the animals as entertainment was seen then as part of the zoo's mission alongside educating the public and learning more about animals.

In the 1950s, the zoo sent its animals out as ambassadors and entertainers. Lion cubs displayed in the windows of Seattle's premier department store, Frederick & Nelson, drew an enthusiastic crowd of riveted children during the Christmas shopping season.

monkeys as diminutive humans. This explains the exhibit furnishings from the human world that were common in many zoos until they were challenged in the 1970s. At one time Monkey Island included a schoolhouse with a bell that the monkeys could ring.

The zoo survived the Depression, which had threatened its very existence and required sacrifice and

ingenuity on the part of the staff. By 1940, things were looking up. But after the attack on Pearl Harbor in late 1941, the U.S. suddenly entered World War II, and the zoo faced some new challenges right away.

CHAPTER FOUR

MORE MONEY, MORE KIDS, MORE ANIMALS

AFTER WAR WAS DECLARED, WPA workers, responding to the need for soldiers and defense workers, left the zoo with only two days' notice, leaving projects unfinished. Some zoo staff members also went off to war. Temporary employees were hired to take their places, but getting them properly trained put pressure on the small staff. A teenaged Melvina Kuempl was hired to fill in for a zookeeper, and as the first woman zookeeper in Seattle, she was considered a novelty. (It would be another 25 years before a woman would once again be part of the animal-keeping staff at Woodland Park Zoo.)

The zoo was made ready for possible enemy action. An anti-aircraft gun site and a searchlight were placed in what later became the North Meadow. The zoo put firefighting equipment in all buildings and had a locker with firearms. There were also preparations for escaping animals if the zoo was attacked. Venomous reptiles were eliminated from the collection, and deer had their antlers removed. The carnivore cages were expected to withstand enemy action.

The catchphrase of the day was "There's a war on, you know." Materials were diverted to the war effort, and there was no new construction, just needed repairs.

BELOW: Zoo staff in front of the Primate House, ca. 1940: Ed Johnson at far left; keeper Gene Chriest, fourth from the left, back row; Frank Vincenzi, fourth from the right, back row. The lone woman, center back, is Margaret Wheeler, who was the administrative mainstay of the zoo for many years.

LEFT: Sultana tiger cubs in the Feline House Grotto, circa 1950s.

Gasoline and tire rationing, as well as mileage restrictions, were imposed on all City departments. Getting certain seeds for birds and fruits and vegetables for other animals became impossible, and substitutes had to be found.

But the zoo had more visitors than ever. Gasoline rationing had put a limit on out-of-town excursions, so people had to find recreation closer to home. There were a lot of military personnel at the zoo as well. Gus Knudson wrote, "Woodland Park Zoo has always been a great attraction for service men. Many of the boys and girls now in uniform are from the inland states and have never had the opportunity to see a zoological park. . . . Hundreds of them throughout the year have been seen at the monkey island watching the antics of these very amusing creatures." (Annual Report to Seattle's Board of Park Commissioners, 1943)

Family life changed. With fathers at war and mothers joining the workforce, it became fairly common for children to be dropped off at the zoo. Unsupervised adolescents had become a concern everywhere, and the zoo was no exception. Teenagers were throwing rocks at squirrels, shooting at caged animals with BB guns, using slingshots, throwing bottles, and climbing into paddocks. Some visitors were even giving monkeys cigarettes and lighted matches.

The Wallingford Police Station dispatched uniformed personnel to help, but the problems continued. For years, Knudson had recommended that the zoo be enclosed by a gated fence, but the City balked because of concerns about public acceptance and costs.

When the war ended in 1945, Seattle's Department of Parks and Recreation reactivated plans that had been put on hold for new exhibits and much-needed improvements. A seal pool was completed in 1946, and later became a penguin exhibit. Construction also began on pools for flamingos and swans. The cost of

Zoo director Gus "Doc" Knudson lobbied city hall hard for the zoo and also appealed directly to citizens, revealing his flair for public relations.

pony rides increased from a nickel to a dime, and the Park Board approved the installation of a miniature train concession, with 10 percent of the gross receipts to go to the City.

Gus Knudson had worked at the zoo for 40 years, and he retired in 1947 at the age of 67. Despite his fun-loving persona, Knudson had been frustrated for years. During the Depression and war years he'd had to make do with a small staff and a collection of animals received almost entirely through donations. Most animal food also came through donations and typically required that zoo employees leave the grounds to pick it up. Knudson was also disgusted by a lack of funding from the City, and by visitors' mistreatment of animals.

On June 4, 1947, an autopsy of Roly Poly the seal revealed that his stomach contained more than 100 copper pennies; three nickels; 84 aluminum, plastic, and brass tax tokens; one brass lapel insignia of the army's Second Infantry Division; two tiny pieces of steel; and a collection of metal washers and buttons. Gus Knudson had reported the stomach contents to the press in the hope of stopping some visitors' cruel practice of tossing items into the animal habitats for "fun." The cause of death was determined to be aluminum poisoning from the tax tokens. The death of Roly Poly came after the recent deaths of 16 bald eagles who had eaten wire staples thrown at them.

Throwing objects at the animals is a form of cruelty that has been associated with humans' desire to interact and engage with animals, to get the animals to make eye contact with them, and to see them move around. It has been a consistent problem since the beginning of public zoos.

Knudson's farewell remarks were front-page news. He called the zoo "a prison and a disgrace to the city." He blasted previous Park Boards for micromanagement and the City of Seattle for its stinginess. He said, "I've been the goat all those years. I've had to send keepers out begging for food for the animals. . . . If Seattle can't afford to feed its animals without . . . the keepers running around begging for food, it's an outrage!" (*Seattle Daily Times*, August 21, 1947) He also spoke up about the cramped conditions for some of the animals and the antiquated design of some of the zoo's older exhibits. The public listened, and support began to build for a bond issue that would fund the zoo properly.

Knudson was succeeded by head keeper Edward J. Johnson, who traded in his zookeeper's uniform and cap for business suits and ties and got right to work. Johnson was able to make big changes because Knudson's farewell speech had made a significant impression on the public and because after the hard years of Depression and war, America was entering a decade of great prosperity. Most buildings and enclosures at the zoo had been built during the first two decades of the 1900s. A 1948 bond issue was approved by voters, and $800,000 was earmarked for the zoo. Johnson was ready to make good use of it. He had worked at the zoo continuously since 1928, except for two years during World War II, when he had served in the Pacific Theater.

Johnson had grown up in the Ballard neighborhood. As a boy, he had volunteered to feed and give water to zoo animals. He lost his mother at age 5, and his father at 10, and was raised by siblings and other relatives in a close-knit family of Swedish Finns. In his teens, he went to work in a logging camp on the Olympic Peninsula and sent money home to the family. While there, he memorized poems by Robert W. Service, the popular poet of the Klondike gold rush known as "the bard of the Yukon." Years later, Johnson entertained the family with his Christmas recitations of "The Cremation of Sam McGee."

Edward J. Johnson (left) with Gus Knudson. Johnson became the second director of Woodland Park Zoo in 1947.

He was an avid reader and an eager lifelong learner, with a particular interest in scientific journals, evolutionary biology, and innovations at other zoos. He spent his life educating himself and others.

He also valued hands-on learning. He had read or heard that when boa constrictors squeeze the rib cage of a prey animal, they tighten down a little more each time the constricted animal breathes out. With keepers nearby, he wrapped a boa constrictor around his own rib cage and allowed the snake to tighten with each of his exhalations until he gave a signal to have the snake pulled off.

Throughout his career, Ed Johnson would bring animals home with him if they needed special care. When newborn felines were rejected by their mothers, Ed Johnson and his wife, Ruth, would bottle-feed them around the clock, much to the delight of their children Jeannette and Eddie.

Jeannette Johnson Reynolds recalled rushing home from elementary school to her Ballard home at

Zoo director Ed Johnson with one of his favorite friends, Wide Awake, in 1948.

Ed Johnson's children Eddie and Jeannette loved it when their father cared for newborn animals in their home.

lunchtime to check on the welfare of a series of cubs. Sadly, they didn't all make it. They included lions, tigers, black panthers, and leopards. When the black panthers were in residence, her mother installed a board blocking the door from the linoleum-floored kitchen to keep them off the carpets.

Reynolds also remembered lying in bed and hearing a group of nocturnal flying squirrels racketing around in their cages in a downstairs room.

In 1948, construction began on the zoo's first administration building with an office, keepers' locker room, first-aid room, and small auditorium. The zoo had never had a proper sheltered work space for employees. That same year, zebras debuted at Woodland Park Zoo. It was the first time in the zoo's history that the City had authorized money to buy animals.

The Elephant in the Back Seat

· · · · · · · ·

When Ed Johnson's daughter Jeannette was a toddler, Morgan Berry, a former zoo employee who later went out on his own as an animal trainer and trader, pulled up one day in front of the Johnson home in Ballard. He had removed the back seat of his car to make room for a baby elephant that he wanted to sell to the zoo. Flabbergasted neighbors gathered quickly to see the elephant in the Johnsons' front yard.

The nonchalant Berry was also behind the wheel a few years later, on May 23, 1958, when elephants in his care ended up on another front lawn. A trailer with four of them overturned at the corner of Phinney Avenue and 67th Street, near the zoo, damaging a car. The elephants were uninjured and wandered about briefly, but were walked to the zoo through a crowd of gaping passersby. Mrs. F. E. Ungar, who lived near the corner, said, "I've never seen anything like it. Imagine elephants all over my front lawn!"

Morgan Berry had to remove the back seat of his car to make room for the young elephant, 1952.

Jeannette Johnson, aged two, holds elephant trainer Morgan Berry's hand in front of her house while his baby elephant enchants the neighborhood kids in 1952.

In 1979, Berry was found dead at his animal farm in Woodland, Washington. His body had been trampled and tossed for hours by a five-ton bull elephant. It wasn't clear if the 68-year-old Berry had suffered a heart attack or if the elephant, Buddha, had killed him, but the condition of the body made it impossible to determine. Berry's long and colorful career included many international trips to acquire exotic animals.

The innovative bear grotto, completed in 1950, was a huge improvement over the barred cages and dark pits that had been used in zoos up to that time.

During his first year as director, Ed Johnson played a major role in the design of the Aviary, and his signature appears on the blueprints. With this new Aviary, Woodland Park Zoo entered the modern era in accordance with the goal of "modernization," which was central to the purpose of the zoo's bond funding.

Many more buildings were to come in the decade that followed, and older structures such as the 1911 Primate House were updated, making use of technical advances in heating, ventilation, and air-conditioning systems, providing more comfort for the animals.

At $242,853, a 1950 bear grotto was the largest item on the improvement list and the most expensive project in the zoo's history. Ed Johnson and Park Engineer W. C. Hall had visited 22 zoos, and all the grottos they had seen were built on a hill, with dens dug into the hill, making it damp and dark for the animals.

Johnson and Hall placed dens in a circular configuration on flat land, with viewing grottos circling the outside. The resulting grottos were a vast improvement for bears that had previously been exhibited behind bars or in pits and allowed bears to find shade or sun in any given enclosure.

In 1948, the zoo received more than 150 gifts of animals, totaling over 275 individuals. Johnson made it clear that the zoo had the last word on donations, writing, "We reserve the right to screen the donations to determine their value as an exhibit."

He was also working hard to fine-tune the collection. Soon after he became director, Johnson traded a spare kangaroo to the Calgary Zoo for two pelicans, a wild dog, and some black foxes. In 1953, tigers Tongou and Sultana were brought to the zoo, where they eventually produced a total of 54 offspring. Forty of them survived, and many were born in litters of five. A building to house kangaroos and giraffes was completed in 1952.

In 1951, a guide and speaker program was inaugurated without any official funding. It was used to build the case for education as a legitimate public service that required staffing. In 1952, the City approved the new position of guide-naturalist. The zoo's publications program also began in 1952. "The Ark," a one-page biweekly information bulletin, was put together by zoo staff. It featured events at the zoo, and included natural-history information on the zoo's animals.

In 1950, a special children's concession known as Kiddyland was placed at the zoo in an area near what later became the South Parking Lot. It had a merry-go-round, Ferris wheel, rocket ride, boat ride, and miniature train, which ran on 2,179 feet (.4 mile) of track. The children's railroad was called Buffalo Barn and Southern because it ran between the bison barn and southern portion of the zoo.

The postwar baby boom was on, and Kiddyland was soon crawling with kiddies. Parking was already a problem, and Kiddyland's popularity had made the problem worse. People complained that lines and waiting times were too long and that children became so enthralled with the rides that they refused to move on into the zoo with their families. In 1953 and 1954, Kiddyland was moved farther inside the zoo, and the

area that it had occupied was converted to parking. Two new lots were also added on Phinney Avenue.

There were improvements behind the scenes, too. Isolation and necropsy facilities were built in 1953. The isolation facility was used to quarantine new animal arrivals and to isolate sick animals. The old facility, which Johnson called "unsightly and pitifully inadequate," was demolished. Even though the zoo did not have its own veterinarian on staff, there was a minor laboratory facility with space for X-ray equipment. By this time Johnson had already established a cooperative working arrangement with Dr. S. P. Lehman, director of the Seattle-King County Department of Public Health, and his veterinary staff.

Ed Johnson was presiding over the zoo's most dynamic period of growth and improvement, and there was much more on the agenda.

Ed Johnson feeds the seals in their updated pool, 1946.

Form Follows Function:
The Zoo Embraces Mid-Century Modern Design

• • • • • • • •

The Aviary, built during the first year Ed Johnson was zoo director, was an excellent example of the modernist design approach characteristic of many zoo buildings constructed after the war and for the next 20 years. It lacked the ornamentation and curves found on older buildings such as the Primate House.

The new emphasis was on functionality. Most interior surfaces were smooth and easier to clean and maintain. Exteriors had clean lines and angles, and hedges were pruned in rectangular forms that harmonized with the lines of the building.

Ed Johnson worked closely with Parks Architect A. V. Peterson on plans for the Feline House. Most zoos with simi-

lar facilities in the U.S. had large lobbies from which to view the animals. Johnson and Peterson saved money by designing a covered corridor that eliminated glare and reflection while at the same time providing overhead shelter for visitors. Using glass as a physical barrier between animals and visitors was new—made possible by advances in "safety" glass. Since the glass could still be damaged by extreme impact, a steel curtain was installed that could be dropped into place.

With glass-fronted cages, the Feline House was one of the first of its kind in the country. The interior walls were lined

The Aviary opened on December 5, 1948.

BELOW: The new covered observation area in the Feline House was well suited to Seattle's rainy climate.

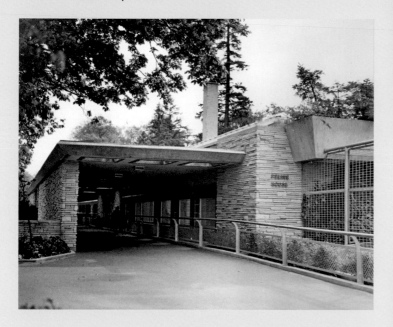

ABOVE: Steel furnishings and tile in glass-fronted exhibits at the Feline House made it easier to keep surfaces clean.

with smooth tiles; resting platforms were built of steel. These relatively nonporous surfaces were durable and much easier to clean than wood, plaster, and porous concrete.

The Feline House went on to exhibit meerkats, fennec foxes, keas, and Komodo dragons, testifying to the flexibility of the building's original design. Nearly exact copies were built at other zoos.

The angular, architectonic forms of this design era were extended to outdoor grottos connected to the Feline House. There was no pretense of naturalism in the "rockwork," but the size, location, and arrangement of these forms allowed animals to select from a variety of locations and microclimates.

RIGHT: Concrete forms in outdoor exhibits connected to the Feline House were provided in various sizes and heights above the ground to give the animals location choices.

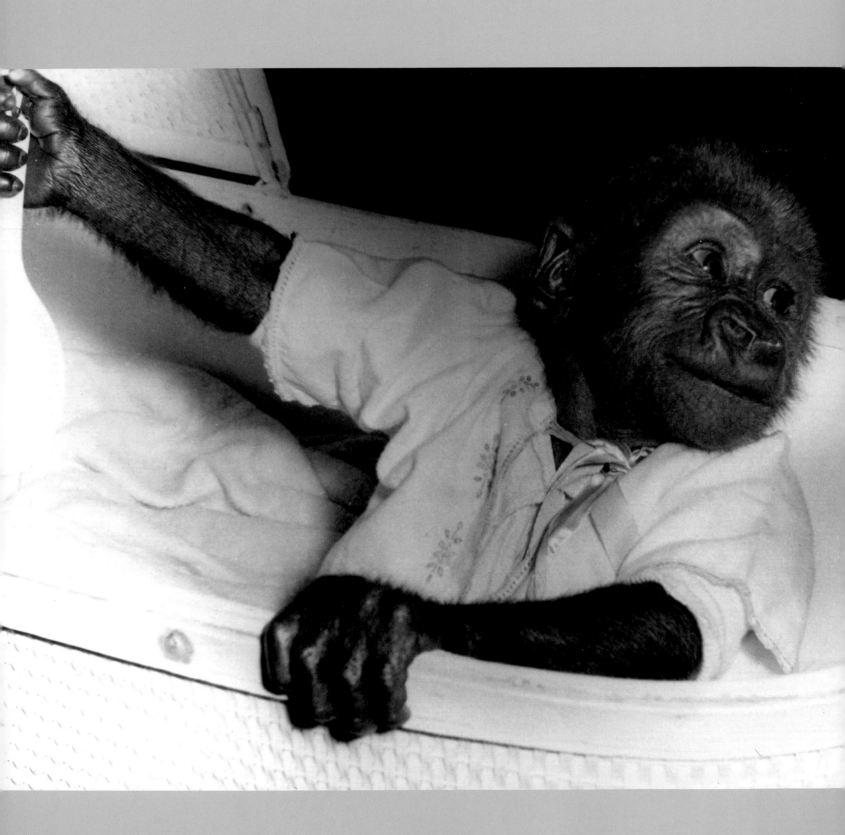

CHAPTER FIVE

BOBO, BUTTONS, AND ELMER

THE BIGGEST NEWS IN THE 1950s was the arrival of a gorilla named Bobo. Other zoos were also interested in Bobo, and his purchase price of $5,500 was more than the zoo had ever paid for an animal. Zoo director Johnson said the high price was justified because Bobo would "undoubtedly prove to be a star attraction," and he was right.

Bobo was more famous than any local politician or celebrity, and his name sometimes appeared as a write-in candidate for mayor or city council. A nostalgic 1981 profile in the *Seattle Weekly* said, "Bobo *was* Seattle, and Seattle was infected by a mad passion, Bobomania."

Bobo was placed in the Feline House, but the youthful creature was already strong enough to shatter the grate above his living area and would soon be strong enough to break down the doors. Johnson appealed for the funds needed to build a Great Ape House.

LEFT: Bobo, here in his human bassinet and sporting the classic baby layette of the 1950s, began his life in a private home.

The Great Ape House was completed a few years later, just in time to accommodate a female gorilla, Fifi, with whom it was hoped Bobo would mate. (The Great Ape House also housed orangutans and chimpanzees.) The occasion was marked by newspaper stories with headlines such as "Park Board Sees Sobbing Bobo, Fussy Fifi Enter New Love Nest" and "Bobo, Fifi Begin Honeymoon in New Zoo Apartment."

Fifi remained with Bobo for the rest of his life. Stories about the fact that they never mated were a regular newspaper staple. Fifi occasionally showed some interest, but Bobo never did. Ed Johnson was quoted as saying, "If she ever gets her hands on a pencil and paper, she's going to write a letter to Dorothy Dix," a popular advice columnist. Bobo was described as being more interested in entertaining his human visitors on the other side of the glass.

While Bobo was undoubtedly the star, there were other new animals to see. In 1954, a male reticulated giraffe named Duke became the first giraffe to be exhibited anywhere north of San Francisco.

The Great Ape House opened in 1957.

A female giraffe named Duchess arrived at the zoo the following year. Both giraffes were donated by Seattle car dealer S. L. Savidge. When Duchess died a few years later, Savidge donated Duchess II.

In 1955, the zoo acquired a sea otter—a first for any American zoo. Very little was known about the species. The zoo and the U.S. Fish and Wildlife Service studied the otter's feeding habits and behavior, the zoo's first collaborative research project.

All over America, rooftops were sprouting antennas, and families were gathering around boxy black-and-white television sets. KCTS, Seattle's educational channel—later a PBS affiliate—began broadcasting in 1954, and in 1955, the station began presenting a half-hour program called *Buttons and His Buddies* every Wednesday at five o'clock, starring Buttons, a baby gibbon. It also featured Ed Johnson, Jack Alexander—the zoo's one-man education department—and Frank Vincenzi, who trained Buttons. They brought animals to the studio and answered children's questions. The zoo's animals were also shown on commercial stations KOMO and KING. In 1956, the zoo produced its first guidebook, *Who's Who at the Zoo*.

The zoo had been dramatically transformed during the 1950s with a new complex of bear grottos, a modern Feline House, Aviary, Ape House, Seal Pool, administration building, Pony Barn, Flamingo Exhibit, and a Giraffe and Kangaroo House. Operations were modernized under Ed Johnson, who had been a keeper for many years and knew that modern materials, equipment, and disinfectants could make the keepers' work easier and more effective.

The popularity of zoos was growing, and they were beginning to take on more of an educational and scientific role. They were supported in these efforts by the American Association of Zoological Parks and Aquariums—later named AZA—a professional organization devised to set standards and facilitate coordination among zoos and aquariums. Ed Johnson served on its board and was elected president in 1958.

By the 1960s, sea otters would be a main attraction.

After Johnson's successes at the zoo, the Park Board promoted him to Superintendent of Parks in 1960, with responsibility for all of Seattle's parks. (Johnson's predecessor, Paul V. Brown, went reluctantly, saying, "I don't beat my wife. I've never been arrested. I'd like to have some reason why I was dismissed." (*Seattle Post-Intelligencer*, May 27, 1960)

The *Seattle Times* editorialized that the appointment was good news, writing, "Although sometimes it is helpful to import executive talent from afar, we are pleased to see a local man of Johnson's ability and knowledge of local problems win the superintendent's job." (*Seattle Times*, January 29, 1961)

Like Johnson, the zoo's new acting director, Frank Vincenzi, had loved animals from boyhood and began his career at Woodland Park Zoo as a keeper. He was born in 1912 to Italian immigrant parents in Black Diamond, Washington, a small coal-mining town in King County. His father worked in the mines, and the family also took in boarders, from whom Frank and his brothers learned their first English words.

In 1922, the family moved to the Georgetown neighborhood in Seattle. During his senior year at Cleveland High School, Vincenzi had to drop out to help support the family, as Ed Johnson had done. He went to night school at Broadway High School so he could graduate. Vincenzi began his career at the zoo in 1930, working in the pony ring and butchering horses for the zoo's meat supply. He later said he almost quit the first day because he hated participating in the butchering. He rode the streetcars three hours a day from Georgetown to the zoo and back again. Eventually he moved closer to the zoo, and by 1954, he was zoo foreman.

Facing danger calmly was part of being a keeper. In the early 1940s, Vincenzi was bitten by a rattlesnake. He removed the fangs from his finger and

Frank VIncenzi, like Ed Johnson before him, was a lifelong animal lover who worked his way up from keeper to leadership of the zoo, in 1960.

fetched antivenom from the medicine cabinet, but he dropped the glass syringe on the concrete floor, where it shattered. Spotting a piece of string under a bench, however, he managed to fashion a tourniquet, slice the wound open with a razor blade, and suck out the venom, then waited at Harborview Hospital while they spent more than an hour searching for antivenom. Undaunted, Vincenzi was later pictured in the local press holding a rattler he had rounded up in the wild on his own time to add to the Snake House.

A polar bear named Mischa made her first public appearance in time to fascinate tourists coming to Seattle during its World's Fair in 1962.

Bobo—The Early Years

Before coming to the zoo, Bobo had been the subject of a *Life* magazine story and a segment of the television show *You Asked for It*. He had also appeared regularly in local and regional newspapers.

Bobo was born in what was at the time French Equatorial Africa. In July 1951, when he was about two weeks old, he was captured by an American gorilla hunter named William "Gorilla Bill" Said. Gorilla Bill placed the infant gorilla in the care of his mother in Columbus, Ohio.

Meanwhile, Bill Lowman, a divorced fisherman, was living with his parents and three young daughters—Sue, Toni, and Claudia—in Anacortes, Washington. He had owned some unusual pets in the past, including a spider monkey. Now he wanted a chimpanzee. When he traveled to Gorilla Bill's home in Columbus, he found out that the Saids didn't have any chimps, but they did have a four-month-old western lowland gorilla. Lowman couldn't resist and purchased Bobo for $4,000.

Bobo quickly learned how to open doors and latches.

Before coming to the zoo, Bobo appeared at an Anacortes gas station for a 1953 *Mobil Dealer News* article.

Bobo joined the Lowman household in December 1951. Bill's mother, Jean, bathed him daily and rubbed him with olive oil to keep his skin soft. She diapered him and dressed him in human clothes as he progressed from bottle-feeding to eating solid food at the table with the rest of the family. Bobo learned to feed himself and was partially toilet trained. Every night he slept with Jean and her husband, Raymond.

Bobo went to drive-in movies with the family, had ropes and tires to swing on, and roughhoused with neighborhood children. He learned to open latches, turn lights off and on, roll car windows up and down, and blow the car horn. He investigated just about everything, and with his increasing strength, he destroyed dishes, records, telephones, and furniture. Occasionally, he would bite someone. The Lowmans began to doubt whether it would be possible to keep him much longer.

Jean read books on gorillas and wrote to people in similar situations for advice. She thought that Bobo could learn to live like a human if only she could learn how to train him. However, nothing seemed to work, and when the Lowmans built a separate room for him, Bobo seemed lonely and depressed.

Finally, they decided it was time to sell him. Bobo was two and a half years old and weighed 60 pounds when he moved to Woodland Park Zoo. Though some other zoos in the country might have been better equipped to take a gorilla, the Lowmans wanted to keep Bobo within visiting distance.

Bobo celebrates his fifth birthday with his human family members Raymond Lowman and Claudia Lowman at Woodland Park Zoo, July 1956.

Bobo arrived at the zoo on December 6, 1953, wearing a jacket, T-shirt, trousers, and suspenders. Film footage shows Bobo hugging the Lowman girls inside his cage. For the Lowmans, this was similar to putting a human family member in an institution. Bobo's human clothes were removed, and at the zoo he was no longer fed at a dining room table.

Jean had planned to stay with Bobo for a few days but ended up staying at the zoo for more than two weeks—first on a couch inside his cage, then in nearby quarters as she tried to get him used to his new surroundings. Bobo's early socialization and his "humanization" by the media continued for the rest of his life. Every year, his birthday was a huge media event. While cameras clicked away, Bobo routinely demolished his birthday cake, much to the crowd's delight.

Claudia Lowman, one of Bobo's "human sisters," reflected on her memories of Bobo's fifth birthday:

I remember the occasion—Bobo's birthday party at the zoo. Here I am (see photo) with a cake for Bobo. Actually, Stan Boreson [the host of a local children's television show] brought the cake, and Stan and his cameraman wanted some good footage for Stan's kids' show, but Bobo was much more interested in his "family" who had come to visit than in a cake.

Frank Vincenzi unbags a reticulated python in one of the Feline House interior cages.

About 10 million people came to town for the fair, and many of them visited the zoo. Visitors could see the zoo from rubber-tired trams called zooliners.

President John F. Kennedy was supposed to be in Seattle at the very end of the fair in October, but he begged off because of "a heavy cold." Later, it was revealed that he was deep into the beginnings of the Cuban Missile Crisis. When the crisis—the most dangerous time of the Cold War—became public knowledge, Vincenzi announced that in the event of a nuclear attack, zoo staff would destroy venomous snakes using cyanide gas or chloroform.

The zoo was making progress on its list of clean-up projects. The old cages with cement walls and steel bars that once housed bears were finally demolished, 11 years after the bears had been moved to their newer grottos. Some of the zoo's free-ranging peafowl had taken up residence in and around the old cages, and when they were torn down, the birds dispersed and some of them wandered through surrounding neighborhoods. Vincenzi eventually asked residents to lure the birds into their garages, close the doors, and call the zoo so that keepers could come by and pick them up.

Vincenzi and his staff were eager to make improvements and additions to the zoo, but the Children's Zoo had been put on hold because of the World's Fair and new construction had been substantially delayed. Vincenzi was also concerned about the lack of outdoor space for the zoo's elephants and tapirs. He suggested new structures with "runs" for these animals and also proposed facilities for hippos, rhinos, and antelope species. In 1963, a pool for the elephants—another step toward giving animals' surroundings features of their natural habitat—was built.

Like the forthright Gus Knudson and Ed Johnson before him, Frank Vincenzi let the Department of Parks and Recreation know in no uncertain terms that improvements were needed:

The welfare of our specimens and the whole-hearted acceptance of our modern structures by our visitors, make modernization of the remaining, unattractive and inadequate areas imperative. We cannot over-emphasize the desirability of new and modern buildings which would . . . create an awareness of cleanliness and neatness which presently elude our best efforts. (Seattle Parks Department Annual Report, 1962)

Keys to the Animal Kingdom

· · · · · · · ·

During the 1960s children often arrived at the zoo with their very own zoo key,
part of a program called Talking Storybooks. The zoo sold special plastic zoo keys shaped like elephants.
Visitors inserted the elephant's trunk into mounted boxes installed outside exhibits, which then
produced a recorded jingle and information about animals in the line of sight. About 5,000
elephant keys at 50 cents each were sold in the first four and a half months.

The key activated a recorded message at more than 40 exhibits in 1960. Kids loved these keys, even into adulthood. One animal-loving young lady on Mercer Island remembered keeping hers in her jewelry box as a precious item. Decades later, some baby boomers still had theirs as a memento of childhood.

Woodland Park Zoo was one of the first to install these devices, and by the end of the following year, the systems had been installed in more than 20 zoos. The tapes eventually broke or wore out and had to be replaced, and the system was removed by the end of 1974.

Zoos had always seen themselves as providing amusement for children, like circuses. But now they were moving toward a more educational approach. The demand for education programs continued to increase. Many of the presentations given by the zoo's single education staff member, Jack Alexander, were school assembly programs that included showing live animals. Of course, these programs were in high demand, and not all requests could be accommodated. The zoo stretched its service by loaning animals to schoolteachers—primarily guinea pigs, rats, mice, and rabbits. Jack Alexander had already been donating much of his personal time to respond to as many requests as possible, and the demand continued to soar.

In 1960, funds were allocated for the construction of the Children's Zoo. The Park Board debated, off and on, about whether the children's zoo should be a storybook land with exhibits based on nursery rhymes and fairy tales or something less whimsical and possibly more educational.

Some Seattle-area baby boomers still had their beloved zoo keys well into adulthood.

A wading pool for elephants was built in 1963.

A Casting Call for a Real Live Elephant

· · · · · · · ·

After a child in one of her classes was killed by a car on the way to school, Seattle schoolteacher Dee Gleed started a children's safety program in cooperation with an established National Safety Club campaign that used an elephant mascot named Elmer. KING-TV promoted a fundraising drive to buy Elmer, the Safety Elephant.

Female elephants are much easier to work with than males, and relatively few zoos have adequate facilities for bull elephants. (Sexually mature bull elephants go through periods of aggression called musth that in the 19th century led to brutal treatment of male circus elephants, the deaths of trainers, and on one occasion, the derailment of a moving train engine by an escaped elephant named Hercules.)

Elmer would have to be a female. She arrived at Boeing Field on June 14, 1956, on a Flying Tiger Line plane. She was greeted with a sugar lump from the blonde Miss Flying Tiger, Pearl Steeves, who wore a form-fitting tiger skin print costume that included a long tail and pumps with high heels. (*Seattle Times*, June 14, 1956)

Elmer was used to remind children—who generally walked to school by themselves in this era—to cross streets safely. Ironically, she was not considered very safe by the staff because she was particularly fond of kicking and banging doors with her tusks and frequently had infections.

Elmer arrives to great fanfare in 1956.

Using charismatic elephants to reach out to children seemed to be a natural pairing. In the 1950s, the zoo began to offer elephant rides again, using elephants owned by elephant trainer Morgan Berry

CHAPTER SIX

The Last of Bobo, Orangutan Twins, and Human Children Behaving Badly

WHAT BECAME KNOWN as the fabulous fifties had been a decade of progress, prosperity, and optimism with a culture of family fun. This was all reflected at the zoo, with its new, modern buildings, better funding for animals and new projects, and Kiddyland. The sixties, a decade of questioning the status quo and looking at the world in new ways, would be very different, eventually ushering in the zoo's most radical change since Guy Carleton Phinney had started clearing his ridge-top forest.

People were thinking about nature and the environment in new ways. Woodland Park Zoo had been seen as a park that provided recreation, and also promoted education. Frank Vincenzi now promoted the zoo's conservation potential. In 1963, he wrote:

Although the primary goal should be to preserve wild animals in their own natural habitat, zoos must accept responsibility for saving species whose existences are precarious. It is hoped that every consideration will be given to continued expansion of our facilities as a means of saving our seemingly doomed wildlife from extinction and preserving for future generations the opportunity to view and study these animals. (Seattle Parks Department Annual Report, 1962)

The Seattle Zoological Society was founded in 1965, under the leadership of Fred Dulanti and Dr. Walter A. Fairservis, director of the Burke Museum at the University of Washington, who was its first president. Vincenzi said the Society's aim was to promote the educational, scientific, and aesthetic interests of the zoo, but also that part of its purpose was to "promote public understanding of international wildlife and the reasons and methods for its conservation in the modern world."

LEFT: Aerial view of visitors gathering for the opening of the Children's Zoo in June 1967. The rose garden can be seen to the upper left.

Using Zoos to Save Endangered Species

· · · · · · ·

When Frank Vincenzi defined species preservation as an important goal for the zoo in the early 1960s, there was precedent for this idea. In the early 20th century, with the encouragement of Theodore Roosevelt, the Bronx Zoo had been instrumental in bringing back nearly extinct bison.

But there are significant obstacles to preserving endangered species on a large scale. A species needs genetic diversity to survive over the long term. Zoos would have to accommodate large populations with appropriate age and sex ratios. Most zoo professionals now realize that there isn't enough zoo space to save more than a very few species.

Among species that receive recovery support from the Woodland Park Zoo is the golden lion tamarin.

Zoos have, however, successfully bred many endangered species, and individual animals can be released in protected habitats. If they survive to reproduce in the wild, then wild populations can increase in size and genetic diversity. In the 1980s, the U.S. Fish and Wildlife Service in partnership with the Los Angeles Zoo and the San Diego Wild Animal Park began a captive breeding program for California condors, whose numbers in the wild had gone down to nine birds. They were captured and bred, then released into the wild. By 2008, more California condors were flying free in the wild than there were in captivity, and by 2014, there were an estimated 410 birds over a wide range.

Over the years, Woodland Park Zoo has contributed animals to recovery projects for Western pond turtles, golden lion tamarins, Oregon silverspot butterflies, and Oregon spotted frogs. The zoo also works with other zoos and conservation organizations selectively breeding animals to maintain genetically (and demographically) diverse populations in captivity. This has reduced the need to import animals from the wild except when necessary to prevent extinction. By the 2000s, more than 90 percent of the animals in the zoo's collection were born or hatched in captivity.

Even if a species is not endangered, information on successful breeding and care is important to the zoo profession. This is particularly true for a species that is likely to become endangered at some point in the future. In 1963, a Celebes macaque was born at Woodland Park Zoo, the first time that this species had reproduced in an American zoo. Today, the Celebes macaque is listed as critically endangered by the International Union for Conservation of Nature.

The Society had 178 members, with dues of $7.50 for a family, $5 for an individual, and $3 for students. By the end of 1966, membership had grown to 500. Admission to the zoo was free, so members weren't joining to save money on the cost of visiting the zoo. They took the zoo seriously, and wanted to help shape its future.

Through its efforts, 30 women were trained as zoo guides in 1966. This group of trainees was the forerunner of the zoo docent program. Soon, additional classes were organized for more docents.

The Zoo Society would also mobilize public support and raise money. The first fundraising goal was to secure funding for additional phases of the Children's Zoo. Work on this long-awaited project had finally begun. Plans called for a frog pond, areas for monkeys and turtles, and a contact area, which included huge land tortoises and barnyard birds. Also included was a walk-through aviary where there were no barriers between visitors and birds.

In 1965, exhibits included 20 Ecuadorian hummingbirds on loan from local bird enthusiast Jan van Oosten, and the three "jungle rulers": a black leopard, a tiger, and a lion. These young and active animals were all displayed in the same enclosure.

In 1966, outdoor enclosures were added to the Aviary to accommodate more birds. Eight snowy owls and a black leopard called Black Jack Argo also came to the zoo that year. The leopard had been kept as a mascot by the Fourth Infantry Division of the U.S. Army, stationed at Fort Lewis, south of Seattle. Black Jack Argo was donated to the zoo when the division departed for Vietnam. He arrived with a complete set of army personnel records, including discharge papers.

Previous director Ed Johnson had proposed a Children's Zoo in 1948, and in 1967, 19 years later, the first phase finally opened. It was named Foreign Friends Village and also served as the zoo nursery, where baby animals were cared for and displayed. In most zoos it was still common practice to separate infants from their mothers to ensure that they received adequate physiological care. Later, newborns were removed only if their survival would be threatened by leaving them with their mothers.

The Zoo Society had raised money to buy a baby elephant named Bamboo I, who was also kept in the Children's Zoo. Another elephant, 54-year-old Wide Awake, died the day before the Children's Zoo had its official opening. Vincenzi said the elephant was one of the zoo's "oldest and dearest residents."

Bobo was found dead on the morning of February 22, 1968. The iconic ape had died at age 17 without offspring. A postmortem showed that he had Klinefelter syndrome, a failure of his reproductive organs to mature. The zoo received thousands of letters and phone calls from Bobo's many fans. Frank Vincenzi announced that he had died of blood clots in his lungs that might have originated in his left leg, possibly injured during some of his crowd-pleasing antics. Vincenzi said he believed that Bobo's personality was formed by his early life being raised as a human, and that he had a "benevolent look," made eye contact with humans, and was "puzzled and curious" about people.

Staff, volunteers, and the public had a hard time saying good-bye to Bobo, and Vincenzi agreed to have him mounted and displayed at the Museum of History and Industry (MOHAI). Taxidermist Chris Klineburger and his son Kent placed Bobo in an upright position for display. Since gorillas typically walk on their knuckles, there were some who objected to the atypical posture, but Vincenzi pointed out that Bobo often did walk upright and that this was an appropriate way to remember him as a unique individual.

Things Get Out of Hand at the Children's Zoo

· · · · · · ·

Zoo staff member Barbara Berry and Walter Fairservis introduce Bamboo I on opening day at the Children's Zoo, June 9, 1967.

The dedication ceremony for the Foreign Friends Village was held on June 9, 1967. Visitors had waited in line for hours, and the formal ceremony started with a program on the bandstand just outside the south gates. Mayor J. D. Braman, Parks Superintendent Ed Johnson, and members of the Park Board officiated. Music was provided by local celebrity Stan Boreson, an accordionist and children's television show host. An estimated 15 to 20 thousand people poured into the Children's Zoo on opening day. It was a noisy, active event. Bamboo I, the baby elephant, was the most popular attraction. At some point she ran off, but she was retrieved without injuries.

But things soon got out of hand. The Children's Zoo was designed to give children hands-on contact with animals, and some of the children broke quail eggs, threw rocks plucked from a man-made stream at the ducks, yanked on the tail feathers of peafowl, dropped baby turtles on their backs, and pounded away on the shell of an Aldabra tortoise. Some of the smaller animals such as turtles, pigeons, rabbits, and guinea pigs were stolen. Adults behaved badly, too. One woman dug up and carted away a rhododendron plant; another rammed a reporter with a baby carriage.

The following Monday, the zoo stationed a guard at the entrance to control the flow of children and adults, and they were able to accommodate the same number of visitors without incident.

A sense of collective shame settled over Seattle, and most of the animals were returned. Children began policing one another. Two eight-year-old girls rang doorbells and collected $14.39, which they sent to the zoo with a note of apology. Subsequently, *Time* magazine quoted Parks Superintendent Ed Johnson as saying, "The contrast is unbelievable. It's as if the public is trying to deserve its new zoo." (*Time* magazine, June 23, 1967)

The 1967 Children's Zoo opening attracted a big crowd and some bad publicity.

After the removal of Bobo's pelt, the rest of his remains were autopsied and taken to the University of Washington primate center. They were stored in a commercial freezer downtown for several years and then moved to the Burke Museum on campus. When the Burke's freezer stopped working in 1975, the remains were "skeletonized" and used for teaching purposes by the anthropology department at the University of Washington.

Bobo's skull, however, vanished. The mystery of the missing skull was detailed in a 1981 *Weekly* article, which concluded that the skull was in the hands of a local doctor who refused to give it up.

In 1997, MOHAI needed space for a new exhibit and Bobo's mount was put into storage, but by this time it was in poor condition. MOHAI received many inquiries about Bobo, and though the museum had reservations about returning the mount to public view,

Unusual for a gorilla, Bobo, who had begun life being treated as a human, often walked upright.

it finally gave in to public pressure. The Klineburgers vacuumed the mount, repaired minor damage, and repainted Bobo's skin with acrylic paints and leather dye. In July 2000, Bobo was displayed in the center of a glass case filled with memorabilia from his youth: the Mobil gas shirt, his bottle and rattle, a jacket, a T-shirt, and a tiny pair of overalls.

After Bobo's death, three young gorillas were donated anonymously by a Seattle family and some of the zoo's docents. Only one, Nina, lived to adulthood. She went on to give birth to four surviving offspring—three at other zoos—and become a great-grandmother.

Bobo was not the only loss of 1968. The young female elephant purchased the previous year by the Zoo Society and kept at the Children's Zoo also died. She was replaced by Bamboo II.

In February, a female orangutan named Molly also died, but not before giving birth to twins. They were born on February 19, and although Molly interacted with them, she didn't seem to know how to feed them. Nineteen hours after giving birth, she was tranquilized to allow keepers to remove the infants for hand-rearing.

Donated animals continued to arrive at the zoo throughout the 1960s. In 1966, a hippopotamus named Gertie joined the zoo's collection. In 1968, five Humboldt penguins arrived. In 1969, two infant gorillas, Kiki and Pierrot (renamed Pete), were donated by Lucille Johnston. Other animals donated that year included a male ocelot, two California sea lions, mynahs, rhesus monkeys, pigtail macaques, squirrel monkeys, parrots, and an African python.

The 1960s saw big changes in the role of women in society. Employment ads in the newspapers headed "Help Wanted Male" and "Help Wanted Female" were standard and legal until 1968. In 1967, there was only one woman on the staff caring for animals, Barbara Berry, the daughter of elephant trainer Morgan Berry.

Although Barbara Berry worked as an animal attendant, a woman had still not occupied a keeper position since Melvina Kuempl's brief stint during the World War II manpower shortage. In 1968, Betty Bartleson was hired as a nursery attendant to take over Barbara

Berry's responsibilities when Berry was asked to care for the twin orangutans born in the winter of 1968.

Bartleson was hired as a keeper the following year, and this opened the door for more and more women to become zookeepers as the years passed. This was part of a nationwide trend. By 2000, 75 percent of all zookeepers in America were women.

Woodland Park Zoo's senior veterinary technician Harmony Frazier-Taylor, circa 1980s.

Twinkle-Eyed Twins

· · · · · · ·

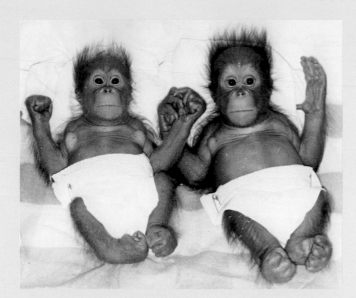

Twin orangutans, Chinta and Towan, were born on February 19, 1968.

When the twin orangutans Towan and Chinta were born, *Life* magazine ran a picture of the babies and noted that the "twinkle-eyed creatures" were the first orangutan twins born in captivity.

The *Seattle Times* and radio station KVI held a naming contest for the orangutans. Their names are Indonesian and mean "master or big boss" for Towan and "love or sweetheart" for Chinta, his sister. Eric Sano was six when he won the naming contest in 1968. He was a lieutenant with the Seattle Police Department when he attended Chinta and Towan's 40th birthday at the zoo in 2008.

Using names from the language of people who share an animal's natural habitat was innovative at the time and has since been incorporated in the zoo's animal-naming policy. Many other animals at the zoo had been named by previous owners, donors, or keepers at other zoos before coming to Seattle. Chinta and Towan's parents were named Molly and Elvis II.

The twins were full-term but small, and spent their first several weeks in an incubator. Towan weighed about three pounds and Chinta less than two pounds. They wouldn't suckle, and zookeepers were worried. There were no veterinarians on staff in those days, so the zoo contacted the University Hospital Center for Premature Infants and the University of Washington Regional Primate Center for help.

Pat Backlund, a young nurse in the neonatal intensive care unit at the University of Washington, came to the zoo to help feed the infants just days after they were born. After a feeding routine was established, Vincenzi asked Marian Davenport, a woman who lived across the street from the zoo, to form and supervise a group of caregivers. Having raised six children, Davenport had experience caring for human infants, and Vincenzi hoped this would translate well to orangutans.

Towan and Chinta were raised by zoo staff and volunteer "babysitters" who came to the zoo to watch them until they were about five years old. Only women with children older than six were allowed to babysit Chinta and Towan because children younger than six are more likely to pick up illnesses that could be transmitted to orangutans.

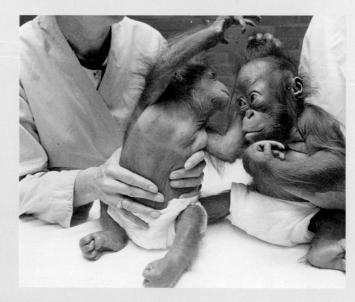

Towan and Chinta were hand-raised by staff and volunteers.

CHAPTER SEVEN

A Bird Lover, the Bartholick Plan, and a Breakthrough Zoo

IN 1968 AND 1969, the Children's Zoo was closed for the winter, because of budget cuts. State Senator Wes Uhlman, who was running for mayor in 1969, called Woodland Park "a bush-league zoo," and the other candidates agreed. The zoo staff of 37 consisted of keepers, two foremen, a guide-naturalist who handled educational outreach, the director, and his secretary. In 1970, the zoo had an annual budget of $453,795.24. At the same time, Chicago's Brookfield Zoo, which received a similar number of visitors each year, had a budget six times as large.

But help was on the way. In 1970, Wes Uhlman was now Seattle's mayor, and he made citizen involvement in the zoo's future a priority. The Seattle Zoological Society, civic groups, and staff from the zoo and the Parks Department were all part of a planning process that included many meetings and analyses, and the Zoological Society hosted an international symposium on "The Zoo of the Future."

LEFT: A mother giraffe and her baby have a captivated audience of school-children behind them.

The voters were on board, too. In 1968, a Forward Thrust bond issue was passed with $4.5 million designated for the zoo, including money to develop a master plan—the first update since the Olmsteds' plan in 1910. Forward Thrust bond issues were part of a series of King County ballot initiatives that a special Forward Thrust committee had developed, including bond proposals encompassing transportation, community housing, water issues, and other publicly financed capital improvements.

The zoo was still trying to complete the projects funded by a 1960 bond issue, and in 1969, the Tropical House, designed for reptiles, opened. In the decade that followed, keepers were able to breed every known endangered reptile species in the zoo's collection.

The old wooden-cottage-like Reptile House was renovated and became the Seattle Zoological Society headquarters.

Architect George Bartholick was chosen to come up with the master plan. He visited more than 25 zoos in the U.S. and Europe and produced a report supplemented by tour files, photographs, and audio-tapes. He didn't like a lot of what he had seen—primates in fake temples, giraffes in buildings meant to look like mosques, and elephants in huge modern concrete structures that dwarfed the animals.

He wrote: "In some zoos I was hardly aware of the buildings, they disappeared or took their place as complementary foils to the animals and plant materials; people do not go to zoological environments to see buildings." He wanted to see bold change, writing, "I would also hold out for a major breakthrough in the exhibiting of animals and zoological environment concepts."

In September 1969, one-man education department Jack Alexander retired after 15 years. He was replaced

by Ernest (Ernie) Wagner and Myron Healy. Their duties included appearances on *Buttons and His Buddies*, then in its 14th year on KCTS Television. It would eventually run for 17 years—one of television's longest-running locally produced children's programs.

Zoo Society docents who had already been helping Alexander assumed full responsibility for zoo tours and also took animals to grade schools three days a week. The zoo was evolving from a city department like any other into one that worked closely with a nonprofit entity and its citizen volunteers.

There was change at the top, too. The previous zoo directors—Gus Knudson, Ed Johnson, and Frank Vincenzi—had all arrived at the zoo as young men and worked their way up from entry-level positions. By the early 1970s, that traditional career path was

The old Reptile House was renovated in 1969 and used as office space by the Seattle Zoological Society.

obsolete. The era of the nationwide search had begun. Two such searches were launched during 1971: one for a full-time veterinarian and another for zoo director.

During the zoo's history, part-time veterinary services had been provided by zoo director and veterinarian Gus Knudson, by the University of Washington, and in the 1960s, by the Seattle-King County Health Department. The Health Department eventually withdrew its support when zoo demands became too much.

Full-time veterinarian Jim Foster started work at the zoo in the middle of 1971. Foster was born in Fort Dodge, Iowa, and attended Iowa State University, where he earned his doctor of veterinary medicine degree in 1954. After serving in the Army veterinary corps in France and Yugoslavia, he returned to Iowa as a small-animal practitioner. In 1960, he moved to the Seattle suburb of Bellevue, where he practiced for 11 years before joining the zoo's staff. He was a skilled falconer and an accomplished mountain climber.

Foster's first six months at the zoo featured some high-profile activity. Gorilla Fifi, the late Bobo's platonic companion, was sent to Honolulu Zoo. Elephant Elmer, who had been acquired in 1956, died at an estimated age of 17. And a fundraising drive was initiated to buy Watoto, an African elephant born in the wild in Kenya in 1969 or 1970. She arrived at the zoo in 1971.

The search for a zoo director took longer. Frank Vincenzi had been working as acting director and had never gone through the formal civil-service process. Vincenzi said he would help choose the new director and would accept a new position, chief curator, when the new director took over. Vincenzi had been at the zoo for more than 40 years and was nearing retirement. His primary interest had always been working with animals. As a curator, he would be able to focus on his real love: the animals themselves.

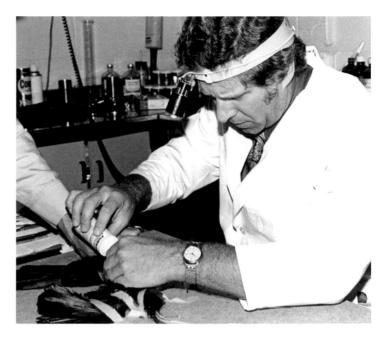

James Foster, DVM, became the zoo's first veterinarian in 1971.

After the nationwide search, 37-year-old Jan Roger van Oosten (the Dutch name is pronounced YAHN van OH-sten) was chosen from 20 finalists. He was working for Texaco as a district supervisor for employee relations and training, but zoology had been his passion since childhood. In fact, family members said that although he had a wide circle of friends and acquaintances, he was "more of an animal person than a people person."

Born in Boston in 1934, he had grown up in France, the Netherlands, and San Marino, California, graduating from the University of Southern California with a degree in international relations and minors in business and zoology. Van Oosten had been on the Mayor's Advisory Committee for the zoo's long-range plan and was a founding member of the Seattle Zoological Society. He had also been a member of the Tacoma Zoological Society and a research associate in tropical ornithology at the Puget Sound Museum of Natural History, at the University of Puget Sound.

Jan Roger van Oosten with Tom the Moose, 1972.

After an expedition to Ecuador, he had published in American and British scientific journals on birds and butterflies there.

Van Oosten started his new job on January 2, 1972. His scope had now broadened from his home aviary to an entire zoo, and he had lots of new ideas.

He promoted the housing of various species together, and said that exhibits should group animals together as they were grouped in nature. One experiment, putting Egyptian plovers in with crocodiles, however, didn't work out as hoped.

He also advocated randomized feeding schedules for zoo animals, believing that feeding animals three square meals didn't properly replicate nature, where variations in food quantity and feeding times are the norm. He also believed that successful breeding was the measure of the proper environment for animals, and like Vincenzi, he felt that captive breeding could play an important role in conserving certain species faced with the threat of extinction.

He worked with Vincenzi to plan assignments so that keepers had time other than when they were feeding or cleaning the exhibits to observe animals for research purposes. Van Oosten also involved keepers in committees concerned with the design of new facilities, graphics, or other interpretive materials.

Van Oosten saw eye-to-eye with George Bartholick, the man behind the long-range master plan. The four-part plan consisted of two interim reports, a schematic plan, and a final planning report, which was issued on August 16, 1971. Bartholick shared his ideas with the zoos he had visited while he did his research. The assistant to the director of the National Zoo in Washington, D.C., Warren Iliff, who went on to a distinguished career as a zoo director in Portland and Dallas, wrote, "The documentation of your tour is brilliant and reflects an in-depth synthesis of the best thinking in the zoo world today."

Bartholick said that the purpose of this new approach was to "enhance the well-being of animals, improve breeding conditions and provide the public with a better understanding of the animals and their habitats." He and van Oosten visualized settings where

This 1970 aerial of the zoo was used as a starting point for planning a new layout. The stark barrier of Aurora Avenue was not lost on Bartholick and van Oosten.

The Man Who Loved Birds

· · · · · · ·

Van Oosten was the son of an amateur ornithologist, and began caring for birds when he was nine years old. He started with pigeons and went on to lovebirds, finches, Australian parakeets, cockatoos, doves, quail, and pheasants before specializing in parrots. As an adult, he built enclosures for birds in the backyard of his home on Capitol Hill in Seattle, furnishing them with live plants and naturalistic perches.

There were birds inside the house, too. Some flew freely through the rooms of the family's home. One of van Oosten's three children, Roger, said that he was about 10 years old before he realized that garages were intended for cars rather than birds—and that the family probably missed a lot of phone calls because they thought they were hearing a parrot's imitation of a ringing phone rather than the real thing.

Besides actual birds, van Oosten collected thousands of bird prints and dozens of bird lithographs, bird statues, bird posters, bird shirts, bird mugs, and bird salt and pepper shakers. Any kind of bird item was a potential addition to his collection, but he was especially partial to parrots.

Van Oosten was an avid reader of scientific journals and particularly eager to learn more about the natural habitats and behaviors of bird species in captivity. His library of about 8,000 books was full of his notes in the margins and on loose papers tucked between the pages.

He was particularly fond of the writings of Jean Delacour, a celebrated ornithologist and a former operator of the Bronx Zoo. Delacour, noted for his studies of rare species, combined scientific rigor with an unabashed enjoyment of birds for their sheer beauty and style. Perhaps as a reflection of his own enjoyment of colorful birds, van Oosten often dressed in colorful clothing—loud ties and plaid trousers.

Marion and Jan van Oosten with a few of their favorite friends.

animals would be displayed in family or other compatible groupings, and in landscapes similar to the animals' natural habitats. This usually meant using plantings, but van Oosten's idea for exhibiting a barn owl within an actual barn was another example of this concept.

Barriers would be either water-filled moats or fencing concealed by vegetation. This wasn't a new concept; it had been used in Germany by Carl Hagenbeck Jr.,

who tested the jumping abilities of many non-swimming species to create his Stellingen Animal Park near Hamburg. It opened in 1907 and used wet and dry moats as well as viewpoints that displayed animals separated by concealed barriers, as if they, as well as human viewers, were part of a contiguous habitat.

The 19 entrances to Woodland Park Zoo would be reduced to one. A bandstand, along with the 1911

George Bartholick unveils "Phase 1" of his master plan, including a 1,600-foot-long roof over Aurora Avenue.

Primate House and the 1948 Aviary, would be demolished, and the rose garden separated from the zoo itself. Without kiddie rides, monuments, or manicured landscaping, the zoo would be distinct from Woodland Park itself. In fact, van Oosten suggested that Woodland Park Zoo be renamed The Seattle Zoo.

In an article he wrote for the Junior League magazine *Puget Soundings* with the title "The Zoo Changes Its Spots," van Oosten described the future look of the zoo. "There will be no buildings as we know them today. Instead, shelters for the animals will be provided but will be hidden under walks or surrounded by plants, so that they will be almost impossible for the public to see. In the new plan, only the [proposed] nocturnal house, the bear grotto and the feline grotto will remain, and the latter two will be modernized."

It was a far cry from the days when animals in barred cages had begged for peanuts, provided rides for children, performed vaudeville acts, or served as costumed mascots in parades. The most far-reaching part of the Bartholick plan was to undo a radical change to the Olmsted plan. More than a generation earlier,

with citizen support, Aurora Avenue had cut through Woodland Park, dividing it into Lower Woodland Park and Woodland Park Zoo. The Bartholick plan now proposed building a lid over Aurora Avenue and extending the zoo into the portion of Lower Woodland Park that had been separated from the zoo for 40 years.

The lid over Aurora would have clear glass side panels and a 50-foot-high roof of translucent fabric supported by air pressure, similar to a structure used for the U.S. pavilion at the 1970 World's Fair in Osaka, Japan. During the planning process, this proposed building was referred to as the Zoological Conservatory Building.

Van Oosten was a man with a mission—a mission he shared with others. After he became director, there were many late nights at the van Oosten home, where he and George Bartholick worked through the details of what they believed would be a breakthrough zoo, pioneering a radical new design approach that would serve as a blueprint for future zoos. But in May 1972, a citizen group called Save Woodland Park, with a nucleus of 85 active members, became an instant powerhouse on the city's political scene. Its members had other ideas.

The Bartholick plan incorporated a glass-lidded Aurora Avenue. Concept Model, circa 1972.

The Rose Garden

· · · · · · ·

While the Bartholick plan's idea was to eliminate the rose garden from the zoo—and the rose garden did end up outside the zoo's gates—the zoo and the garden have always been connected in some fashion.

The impetus for a Seattle Civic Rose Garden in Woodland Park came from the Seattle Lions Club, the Seattle Rose Society, and later Safeco Insurance, which funded the gazebo. The idea was to come up with a garden that was free to the public and showcased roses that did well in the local climate.

The Superintendent of Parks approved the garden plan, prepared by Howard E. Andrews in October 1922. The 1.8-acre garden at the intersection of North 50th Street and Fremont Avenue North opened in 1924 with 150 varieties of roses.

In 1947, the Seattle Parks and Recreation Department took over managing the garden, the same year it became a nationally recognized All-America Rose Selections test site, a status it held until 2010. As a test site, the garden displayed new rose hybrids before home gardeners could find them at nurseries, giving rose lovers a sneak preview of

The Rose Garden, circa 2016.

coming attractions. After two years of testing, only the best of the test subjects were allowed to remain. Others were yanked out of the beds and destroyed or sent back to breeders for fine-tuning, making room for new test subjects.

Local rose lovers rallied in November 1955, during a freak cold wave, and managed to save many plants that could have frozen to death. In 1995, by which time zoo horticulturists had taken complete responsibility for the garden, the All-America Rose Selections organization judged the zoo's rose garden as the finest of the 137 public rose gardens in the United States.

By 2016, more than 200,000 visitors annually were enjoying 2½ acres of roses on display—including 200 varieties and 3,000 individual bush roses, hybrid teas, miniatures, climbers, and tree roses. Evergreen trees in the garden are pruned into mounded shapes, earning them the nickname "the muffin trees," and garden features include a central fountain—now an annual bed—a frieze by sculptor and sometime Seattle resident Alice Robertson Carr de Creeft, a gazebo, and arbors for the climbers. The garden is a popular spot for weddings, and in February, home gardeners are invited to the annual rose-pruning demonstration.

The Rose Garden, circa 1950

CHAPTER EIGHT

A Lid, Leopards, and Lorises

VAN OOSTEN AND BARTHOLICK were calling for a completely different kind of zoo, although the proposed lid over Aurora, with its spectacular Zoological Conservatory, was clearly an exception to the idea of concealed or subdued architecture. But objections to the Zoological Conservatory weren't about the architecture itself. Much of the opposition to the Bartholick plan and its lid over Aurora came from neighbors who used Lower Woodland Park and wanted it kept the way it was. City officials pointed out that new parks such as Discovery Park, Magnuson, and Gas Works would offset the "general use" loss of Lower Woodland Park when the zoo swallowed it up. Citizen activists weren't buying it. Others objected to the $11.5 million it would cost to implement the ambitious plan. They wanted to see the money used to improve what already existed.

The Save Woodland Park organization began a petition drive against the Bartholick plan. Many local

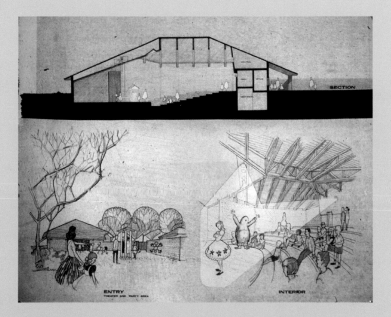

ABOVE: An architect's drawing of the Children's Zoo Theater, 1966. It was completed in 1971.

chambers of commerce and community councils joined the chorus of objections to the zoo's proposed expansion. The Zoo Society responded with its own petition drive in favor of the Bartholick plan. Throughout 1972

LEFT: Snow leopards would become a major attraction at the zoo. Helen keeps watch from the rocks, 2015.

and 1973, van Oosten spent much of his time coordinating with the Zoo Society and providing information to the media, citizen groups, and others as he continued to try to sell the Bartholick plan.

There was also plenty of activity in the existing zoo. The Children's Zoo Theater, the Farm Village, and a new guidebook written by Jack Simmons were all completed in 1971. And on the first day of March, van Oosten woke up his three children at about 2:00 a.m. so they could come with him to the airport to witness the arrival of a pair of snow leopards from Soviet Central Asia.

The leopards had been trapped just a few weeks earlier by Soviet wildlife agents in the isolated Soviet republic of Kirghiz (now the country of Kyrgyzstan)

Helen Freeman began her zoo career as a docent and went on to found the International Snow Leopard Trust.

and had encountered only a few other humans before meeting the van Oostens at the airport. Van Oosten's son Roger later reported that the cats "seemed agitated and were pretty intimidating."

They were named Nicholas and Alexandra after the last Romanov czar and czarina, who had been overthrown by the Soviets who were now providing the snow leopards. At the time, Woodland Park Zoo was one of only 21 zoos in the U.S. and 40 zoos in the world to exhibit snow leopards. Little was known about them. The first known photograph of a snow leopard in the wild had been taken only in 1970, by biologist George Schaller—just a year before the zoo acquired its own snow leopards.

Volunteer Helen Freeman began studying snow leopards shortly after the arrival of Nicholas and Alexandra. Her hard work and enthusiasm have been credited for much of Woodland Park Zoo's subsequent success with snow leopards. Freeman was a docent in 1972 and became the zoo's volunteer coordinator in 1973. She later worked at the zoo as operations manager and became the zoo's first curator of education in 1977.

While employed at the zoo, Freeman founded the International Snow Leopard Trust, a conservation organization. The zoo's first snow leopard birth occurred the following year (1973), and Nicholas and Alexandra went on to produce 12 more offspring during their lifetimes. All but one survived. The first snow leopard to be born at Woodland Park Zoo was named Pushkin, after Russia's beloved poet.

Flying Lessons

Project Babe, named after the zoo's own golden eagle, was the beginning of the zoo's raptor rehabilitation and reintroduction program, in which injured or confiscated birds of prey were cared for in an old guinea pig shed that was repainted and provided with specially timed lighting. With the arrival of veterinarian Jim Foster in 1971, it became possible to treat eagles brought to the zoo with bullet wounds or other injuries. If the birds' injuries weren't too severe and if the birds hadn't become overly dependent on people, they were released in the wild.

The zoo's raptor rehabilitation program—pioneered in 1972—won a prestigious conservation award presented by the American Association of Zoological Parks and Aquariums (AAZPA). The program used radio telemetry to monitor eagles after their release in the wild. Since then, Woodland Park Zoo has rehabilitated and returned to the wild more than 70 eagles and other raptors.

Wild birds with injuries or behavior that made them poor candidates for release were cared for at the zoo. Some were unable to fly over long distances or were imprinted on people before arriving at the zoo. When animals become imprinted on humans and are released in the wild, they often find their way to humans because they associate people with food or other necessities of life. And because imprinted animals have little or no fear of humans, they may move into urban environments where they are injured by vehicles or directly by humans.

In 1972, the zoo launched a raptor rehabilitation and reintroduction program for injured birds.

A record 300 new births were recorded at the zoo in 1973. Closed-circuit television systems were installed in several areas so that many of these offspring could be monitored without unnecessary disturbance. One camera was placed in the raptor barn so that the public could watch prairie falcons incubate their eggs and raise their young. The closed-circuit system was also used to record the birth and development of two polar bear cubs.

By the beginning of 1973, there were 446 mammals (105 species), 735 birds (185 species), 185 reptiles (106 species), and 10 amphibians (10 species). The zoo had only $6,000 a year to purchase animals. The annual food budget was $60,000, with another $20,000 coming as in-kind donations from packers and grocers.

A Walk in the Dark

· · · · · · ·

Zoo visitors had long been cheated of a chance to see animals from a vast number of species in action because the animals were asleep while the zoo visitors were awake, and vice versa. The Nocturnal House created an environment unlike any other, and took the public into a whole new world with bats, big-eyed lemurs, slow lorises, and other seldom-seen species. The animals' daily biological clocks were reversed, so that diurnal

The Nocturnal House used innovative technology and artistic flair to showcase elusive, seldom-seen animals in action.

human visitors were more likely to see them in action rather than deep in sleep under their natural daytime conditions.

In the predigital era, this required complex technology to gradually dim and illuminate areas to simulate dusk and dawn. During the human day, there was just enough lighting for visitors to navigate safely and still see the animals. The animal areas would be illuminated at night when the zoo was closed.

The Nocturnal House was designed by the noted Seattle architectural firm Fred Bassetti and Associates. While other zoos had retrofitted existing buildings to house nocturnal

Lighting, design, and a large mural at the entrance of the Nocturnal House provided a transition space for visitors.

The mixed taxa in the Nocturnal House created some interesting situations. A note from the minutes of a January 2005 supervisors' meeting was headlined: Bat bites armadillo, armadillo chokes bat: Smack Down at WPZ, and read, "A Rodrigues fruit bat and an armadillo somehow engaged one another with the result being that the armadillo rolled into a ball, trapping the bat by the head. It turns out the bat had bitten the armadillo on the nose. The only way to separate the two was to briefly anesthetize (via isoflurane gas) them both. They each then relaxed, were separated and treated. Both seem to be fine today and should return to holding in the Nocturnal building in a couple of days."

The Nocturnal House used backlit graphics, moving images, and audiotapes of crickets to help set the mood for visitors. This was the zoo's first "soundscape." There were also closed-circuit video systems, so keepers and others could observe animals from offices behind the scenes. The Nocturnal House was subsequently renovated with digital upgrades to the exhibit's interpretive systems.

animals, this was the first one designed just for that purpose. Because no natural light would illuminate the exhibits, all the vegetation had to be artificial. Stewart Rodda, a landscape designer who was also a trained fine artist, was contracted to make artificial trees and geologic formations for the exhibits.

Fiberglass was the preferred medium for much of his work. Rodda and four assistants made impressions of rocks at the Riverton quarry, near the Police Department's shooting range, to create rocklike textures in concrete and fiberglass. It was the most extensive use of artificial exhibitry in the zoo's 75 years, and the resulting experience was so intense that some visitors found it overwhelming.

The costs of maintaining such a large collection continued to increase while the operating budget did not, and there were concerns about overcrowding. Furthermore, the Bartholick plan recommended that social species be shown and cared for in group sizes found in nature, whenever feasible. Surplus animals were sold, traded, or sent to other zoos on breeding loans. The zoo's animal inventory was reduced by a total of 100 animals, but species diversity increased as the zoo tried to build reproductive groups of several species new to the zoo. Some of these were to be featured in the Nocturnal House, which was completed in 1974 and was opened to the public the following year.

Caring for animals was undergoing some changes. The era of visitors tossing peanuts and marshmallows to the animals came to an end when a no-feeding policy was established in the spring of 1973, but visitors were still free to feed free-roaming birds or squirrels.

Behavioral enrichment for zoo animals was still in its infancy, and it was unusual for exhibits to be designed to stimulate natural behavior by mimicking natural topography and vegetation. But keepers did scatter food for certain animals to stimulate foraging behavior, and structures were placed in exhibits to keep animals occupied and encourage physical exercise.

By 1973, a merry-go-round had been installed in the gorilla cage, and a slide from Monkey Island had been moved to the outside grotto for gorillas. The orangutans now had a cargo net, so they could spend less time on the barren floor of the Ape House. These objects didn't create the natural surroundings advocated by the Bartholick plan, but they did offer the animals a wider range of behavioral choices and exercise.

The 17-member Citizens Zoo Advisory Committee, appointed by the mayor to coordinate citizen input after the Bartholick plan and its lid over Aurora had caused such a commotion, began to focus on

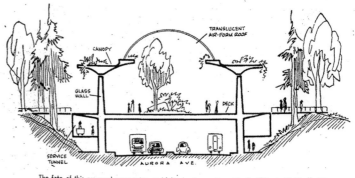

The fate of this proposed conservatory and lid over Aurora Avenu North will be decided by Seattle voters November 5. An initiative on the ballot would doom the lid. A substitute measure would permit construction of about half of the lid and two-thirds of the conservatory. No zoo expansion east of Aurora would be permitted under either measure.

Woodland Park—still a war zone

Fierce debate about the zoo's future marked the tenure of director Jan van Oosten. This newspaper illustration depicted the lid over Aurora that he championed and voters rejected.

funding. The zoo's budget in 1972 was less than $500,000. At that time, the San Diego Zoo, with similar acreage, had a budget that was 10 times bigger. The superintendent of Seattle's Department of Parks and Recreation, Hans Thompson, described the zoo funding as "a starvation budget." The zoo couldn't even keep its concession revenues. They went into the general parks fund.

The Advisory Committee thought the zoo should be autonomous, with its own board of directors, not function as part of the Seattle Parks and Recreation Department. More than half of the zoo's visitors came from outside the city, and the committee suggested it be run and funded by King County or another regional entity.

The Seattle Zoological Society tried to support the zoo through its own fundraising, but the going was tough. In 1972, they sold only 565 family memberships. It was a hard sell because the zoo didn't charge admission. The Zoo Society couldn't offer passes that would save on multiple admission fees to members as it does today. In fact, it would have been expensive to collect admission fees or monitor passes at that time because the zoo still had 19 informal entrances.

Volunteers, however, were donating their time and supporting the zoo's goals of education and research. In 1973 there were 79 active docents, and volunteers were also studying the behavior and nesting of wild prairie falcons in cooperation with Washington's Department of Game and U.S. Fish and Wildlife. In 1974 a new volunteer program provided training for students over 16 years old who were interested in zookeeping, veterinary medicine, or wildlife management, and a new program for coordinating research activities at the zoo was implemented.

Research needs were identified primarily by the zoo rather than by students or volunteers. Veterinarian Jim Foster established a program with the Washington State University School of Veterinary Medicine, giving graduate students an opportunity to work with zoo animals and keeper staff, gaining practical experience.

The debate about the Bartholick plan continued. The new Parks superintendent, Dave Towne, said the basic question was whether to use the $4.5 million from the bond issue to refurbish the existing zoo, or to use it for the first phase of a much more ambitious undertaking. Under the direction of the City, architect Clayton Young came up with a couple of alternative plans—both eliminating the lid over Aurora and expansion of the zoo.

After months of research, planning, environmental-impact assessments, personal appearances with community groups, and countless other meetings, it became clear to van Oosten that the Bartholick plan would not obtain public approval. The City Council approved two measures for the November ballot that van Oosten said would ultimately kill the plan. He submitted his resignation, effective October 15, 1974.

The bird-loving van Oosten didn't go quietly. The *Seattle Times* quoted him as saying, "I think I'd characterize myself as one angry man," and also that he was "violently upset" about the City Council's action. He vowed to continue to campaign for zoo expansion.

Parks Superintendent Towne praised van Oosten for bringing "spirit and vitality" to the zoo, and then appointed zoo veterinarian Dr. Jim Foster acting director. The Bartholick plan was formally rejected by voters in November 1974.

Although van Oosten left after the failed zoo-expansion bid, his influence at the zoo would continue, including his love of birds

CHAPTER NINE

FROM INMATES TO CLIENTS,
FROM HOUSES TO HABITAT

THE VOTERS HAD DECIDED the zoo wasn't going to get any bigger. The pressure was on to align a long list of zoo projects within a more restricted space. Among other things, the City of Seattle and King County discussed developing a regional zoo outside Seattle and converting Woodland Park Zoo into a Children's Zoo. Superintendent of Parks Towne even recommended that the City consider closing the zoo unless a consensus on its future could be reached that would be supported by elected officials.

Bartholick had said something similar in an interim report four years earlier: "I would suggest that the collection and exhibiting of animals goes right to the heart of the question, 'Why have zoos?' Many people feel that if a zoo cannot select, care for and exhibit animals in a healthy, humane, educational and entertaining manner, then it should be disbanded."

After voters rejected the Bartholick plan, Mayor

Wes Uhlman formed a citizens' task force, chaired by Park Board member Cal Dickinson, to come up with a new scaled-down plan. Architect Clayton Young, at Dave Towne's request, developed a concept that demonstrated how the bond projects could be accommodated on current zoo grounds, and provided an alternative basis for the task force's consideration. Architect David Hancocks was named design coordinator for the new plan by Towne. Hancocks had originally been recruited to Seattle to work on the Bartholick plan, but had returned to his native Britain after its failure.

Hancocks' approach had been shaped by personal experience. He was raised in a rural village and, as a boy, explored forests, heath, hedgerows, and wild streams. As an architecture student at the University of Bath in the 1960s, he discovered the newly emerging field of ecology and sought to find a way to combine nature with man-made environments.

He applied for and was offered a job at London Zoo's department of architecture. After the initial

LEFT: Zoos began to change the viewing relationship between visitors and animals. Mountain goat Albert scans the horizon from his favorite perch.

David Hancocks was appointed zoo director in April 1976, shortly after the zoo's long-range plan was approved by Seattle's City Council.

interview, he walked into a zoo for the first time. His first encounter was with a gorilla named Guy, sitting on a concrete floor in a small brick cell. The gorilla had lived alone in that tiny space for 19 years.

Hancocks subsequently discovered the writings of Swiss zoo director and animal psychologist Heini Hediger. One afternoon, he said, he read words that jumped off the page: "The standard by which a zoo animal is judged should be the life it leads in the wild . . ."

Hancocks' responsibilities as design coordinator included recommending consultants to develop the new long-range plan. Over a long lunch with Seattle Design Commission chairman Ibsen Nelsen, Hancocks laid out what he considered to be the essential requirements for the zoo planner—an ability to take an ecological approach and the need to design for wild animals' behaviors as well as their physical and psychological needs. He was surprised when Nelsen recommended investigating landscape architects rather than architectural firms. Landscape architecture in England had traditionally focused on garden design. Hancocks was unaware of the history of ecological emphasis in American landscape studies and design practices.

Inspired by this revelation, the Parks Department and Design Commission interviewed several local firms and proposed that the plan be completed by Jones & Jones, a new Seattle firm. It would be the first time in history that a zoo master plan was created by a landscape design firm.

Many animals were still living in cramped, sterile enclosures devoid of plants and other aspects of natural environments. The grounds and exhibits were often littered with peanut shells, and animals were seen resting or pacing on hard concrete surfaces. Primate exhibits featured metal playground equipment and rubber tires hanging from chains. Most barred cages had been removed by this time, but the exhibits still seemed like human jails.

In the 1970s, notions of how a zoo should house its animals were going beyond simply containing the animal for public viewing, such as in this 1913 polar bear enclosure.

Making Nature the Norm

· · · · · · · ·

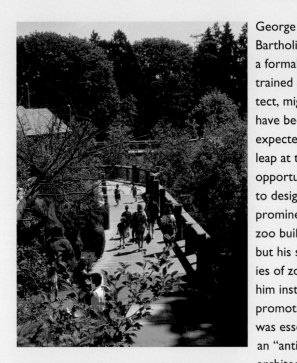

Rather than animals surrounded by people, Jones & Jones argued that the visitors should be immersed in and surrounded by the animal habitats.

George Bartholick, a formally trained architect, might have been expected to leap at the opportunity to design prominent zoo buildings, but his studies of zoos led him instead to promote what was essentially an "anti-architecture" concept. He envisioned a zoo that would be remembered primarily for its animals and habitat landscapes, not for its buildings. Of course some buildings would ultimately be necessary, but the idea was that these should be purposely understated, screened by plants and eventually invisible in the landscape. They should not draw attention to themselves as architectural statements.

Jones & Jones was asked to simulate habitats with no sense of separation between animals and people and to blur the barriers by putting the same landforms and plantings in both the public and the animal areas. The idea was for visitors to feel like respectful interlopers in the wild domain of animals who had wandered into places over which they did not have complete control or dominance. On this more even playing field, animals would be seen in a context that preserved their dignity and inspired a deeper sense of wonder.

Simulating natural landscapes in both visitor and animal areas required an entirely different role for horticulture. At this time, the zoo relied exclusively on City gardeners who worked part-time at the zoo. Zoo landscapes consisted primarily of flower beds, manicured lawns, neatly pruned hedges, and ornamental trees selected for their aesthetic appeal and hardiness rather than their resemblance to species found in an animal's natural habitat.

The term "landscape immersion" was originally coined by Grant Jones of Jones & Jones as he worked on the zoo's plan, and later it became a common term in the zoo profession. Landscape immersion included using plant species from the animals' native habitat, or species that closely resembled them. The team began to refer to these substitute plants as "simulator species," a term that is now also part of the vocabulary of zoo horticulture.

Many of the design guidelines associated with landscape immersion require attention to seemingly small but important details related to human perception and psychology. Certain design techniques are intended to introduce surprise, ambiguity of terrain, or even the illusion of danger.

Regardless of where they are on the food chain, animals ultimately depend on plant life. Characteristic plant types are distributed according to temperature ranges, precipitation, and evapotranspiration rates—the three variables that differentiate bioclimatic zones. These differentiating factors were derived from a life zone model developed by ecologist Leslie Holdridge in 1972 but had never been applied to a zoo.

The Jones & Jones team used the slogan "Nature as the Norm" in their design document. They also studied attributes of the zoo such as sun aspects, drainage, topography, and existing vegetation. This analysis helped determine the optimal location of bioclimatic exhibit zones across the zoo grounds.

In the zoo's early days, few objected to this prison-like appearance, perhaps because it was reassuring that dangerous animals were contained and under control. The zoo's first director, Gus Knudson, along with the press, often referred to zoo animals as "inmates," although this term quickly disappeared from the reports of his successor, Ed Johnson.

Enrichment features such as climbing structures to encourage the natural activity of animals in the wild were often put into man-made exhibit spaces designed with no thought of replicating a natural environment.

In the early 1900s, animal exhibits were simply and honestly called cages, pits, pens, and yards. Off-view areas were referred to as "holding" areas. Given their shared concerns about escapes, locks, and keys, it's not surprising that prisons and zoos used much of the same terminology. Besides changing the look of the zoo, the new approach would also change much of the zoo's internal language and culture.

Exhibits at Woodland Park Zoo had been organized taxonomically through most of its history. Visitors went to separate areas to see different taxonomic groups

such as birds, primates, and reptiles. The zoo had been laid out in large part as a neighborhood of "houses"—the Primate House, Tropical House, Nocturnal House, Great Ape House, Feline House, Elephant House, Reptile (Snake) House, and an Aviary for birds. Most of these buildings were intended to be visible from a distance.

Humans typically think of houses as comfortable places that meet their own physical and psychological needs, but for most animals a house is not a home. Hancocks argued that the idea of providing houses for animals should be replaced with the concept of providing habitat, writing, "All attempts will be made to create situations where the exhibition of the animals can be achieved through a landscape solution, thereby eliminating 'exhibition houses' unless essential."

The Jones & Jones team included designers Grant Jones, Johnpaul Jones, Jon Coe, and John Swanson, with Hancocks as project coordinator, and ecologist and naturalist Dr. Dennis Paulson ensuring that the work was based on solid science.

Grant Jones and Jon Coe had been classmates at the Harvard Graduate School of Design, both graduating with master of landscape architecture degrees in 1966. Coe's master's thesis was titled "Artificial Habitats for Captive Animals," for which he spent a year and a half studying the history of zoos and focusing on animal behavior. Jones' thesis was on regional environmental planning processes.

Coe had studied and organized his thesis into bioclimatic zones or biomes, a concept that became integral to the overall design. Jones & Jones proposed using bioclimatic zones to organize exhibits. In nature, animals and the habitats they occupy are distributed within different bioclimatic zones such as tropical rain forest, desert, temperate forest, and savanna. The idea of mixed-species displays seemed particularly

Some of the zoo's earlier exhibits did strive for habitat, at least in design, if not yet in natural plantings and environments.

appropriate for the zoo's ecological emphasis. Dennis Paulson listed plant and animal species suitable for each exhibit zone. Drawings also showed details such as lines of sight and ways to conceal physical barriers so that views of untrammeled nature would be associated with living animals, even in a zoo.

The planning team also said that certain conditions for viewing animals should be avoided, including "surround views" and "down views." At the bear pits and at Monkey Island, visitors typically surrounded animals on all sides. Especially in the early days, they looked down to see bears groveling for peanuts at the bottom of a pit. The animals appeared conquered, trapped, and diminished. The psychology of humans as captors and animals as captives was reinforced. The new guideline would be to elevate animals to a position at or above human eye level. People would look upward to see animals. And rather than people surrounding animals, animals would surround people—with both immersed in naturalistic landscapes.

Crowds of people can have a huge effect on the sights and sounds of viewing areas. Multiple viewpoints

Multiple viewpoints were designed to break up visitors into smaller groups.

could be used to break up crowds into smaller, less intimidating group sizes. Not only would this give visitors a more intimate contact with nature, but it would reduce stress on animals.

Multiple viewpoints would also give visitors more than one opportunity to see animals moving through an environment. If an animal was hidden from one viewing angle, it might be revealed at another angle farther down the path. Exhibit topography could also be shaped to control sightlines so that visitors didn't see other people, buildings, or service vehicles. It would also be possible to visually make use of landscapes in the background that were not physically within the exhibit.

Jon Coe said the creative process was that he provided the designs for all the exhibits and for the long-range plan, then presented them to Grant Jones, Dennis Paulson, and David Hancocks "and together we discussed and improved them."

The publication of Woodland Park Zoo's "Long-Range Plan, Development Guidelines and Exhibit Scenarios" in early 1976 was not only the first zoo plan developed by landscape architects, it was also the first to declare that animals were the primary clients. Eventually, zoo design and planning became a growth

industry for Seattle firms that spun off from Jones & Jones, taking advantage of the expertise they had gained on Woodland Park Zoo projects.

The plan had been approved by the Design Commission in December 1975, and was adopted by the Seattle City Council in March 1976. Although architect David Hancocks had never imagined he would ever run a zoo, and had no direct experience working with animals, he was offered the job of zoo director and the chance to make the plan reality.

Newly appointed zoo director David Hancocks and his boss, Superintendent of Parks Dave Towne, were clearly taking some risks in 1976 when they called for dramatic changes to zoo exhibitry. They were very conscious of the fact that the Bartholick plan had recently been rejected by voters. However, Dave Towne told Grant Jones of the design firm Jones & Jones, as well as Hancocks, to "feel free to dream." They did.

Hidden barriers in a natural landscape make the views quite thrilling.

"This Amazing Adventure"—Jon Coe Remembers

Jon Coe and a bonobo pause for a moment of reflection.

topography and such. I think Grant also coined the term Landscape Immersion, but we all picked it up so quickly it seemed to just have emerged among the group, so I don't have a clear memory of that moment. Grant was a wonderful project leader with enthusiasm and encouragement for new ideas.

Dennis Paulson had the encyclopedic knowledge of biogeography, ecology and taxonomy. Being a stern scientist, [he] constantly called us on unsupported suppositions and exaggerations, and insisted on full supporting citations and really taught me how scientists think. This is knowledge I've used in over 70 subsequent papers of my own. He also had an amazing eye for typos and his constant checking resulted in the final LRP having zero typos, most unusual for architect's reports.

David [Hancocks'] great contribution . . . was his insistence that . . . "Nature was the model." Because of my extensive thesis research I was tempted to improve upon the existing zoo model, but David wisely insisted on a much more revolutionary approach of going back to first principles and nature.

More than 40 years later, Jon Coe recalled how the team worked together. "I don't see how this amazing adventure would have been possible if any of us had not been a part of it."

He credited "the amazing collaboration and synergy from all of us and our supporting teams," as well as Parks Director Dave Towne's "trust and foresight," as coming together to make it all happen. "There was no one mastermind behind this long-term success," he wrote in 2016.

Grant [Jones] brought the rigorous site analysis and development suitability methodology—all those studies I did overlaying winter and summer shadow patterns on

Coe also remembered Jim Maxwell, Seattle Parks project manager, for both his encouragement and technical guidance "and also for long-term continuity of the vision long after the first projects were opened," and zoo staff members—Jim Foster, Helen Freeman, Violet Sunde, Lorrie Gledhill, and others—who supported some radically new concepts. Forty plus years on, he said, "As a designer I've grown to understand that exhibit management is at least as important as exhibit design for successful outcomes."

CHAPTER TEN

BACK TO NATURE:
THE TRANSFORMATION BEGINS

CONCEPTUAL DESIGNS were already under way for several new exhibits by the end of 1976. In the meantime, improvements were made to some of the older exhibits. In 1977, staff added soil, leaf litter, logs, and plants to the interiors of glass-fronted, hard-surfaced exhibits in the Feline House. This gave the animals natural materials to claw and climb on, taste, smell, shred, dig through, rub against, and scent mark.

Jim Foster, who had gone back to work full-time as zoo veterinarian after serving as acting director, collaborated with the zoo's first curator of education, Helen Freeman, on a document called "Research Policy and Procedure." It introduced a behavioral research policy that was considered revolutionary and supported more natural areas for the animals. Freeman also spearheaded publication of *Applied Behavioral Research at the Woodland Park Zoological Gardens*, a 406-page scholarly book with chapters by zoo staff and papers by 23 students.

The zoo was becoming more sophisticated, but the habits of an earlier era, when zoos were more akin to circuses or carnivals, lingered. Visitors still threw coins into almost every body of clear water for luck or to make a wish. Most other zoos had the same problem.

LEFT: One new idea was to replicate nature by including more than one species in an exhibit.

ABOVE: Director van Oosten with a public-awareness display of all sorts of objects swallowed by animals when visitors do not behave responsibly.

Ingested coins can sicken or kill an animal, and after a caiman swallowed some, the search was on for a staff member with arms that were long and slender enough to reach down the caiman's throat to remove the coins. Finally, volunteer (later zookeeper) Judy Sievert agreed to try, and she succeeded.

Another tradition, visitors feeding the animals, was banned in 1973, but peanuts for human consumption were sold for eight more years after that. As long as peanuts were available, many visitors couldn't resist the temptation to feed them to the animals. When peanut sales finally ended, some of the staff said it was one of the best things that ever happened. Decades of peanut shells covering the grounds and the exhibits had come to an end. (Cigarette butts would continue to litter the grounds until November 1, 2007, when smoking was banned on zoo grounds.)

The zoo's operating budget was still meager compared to that of many other zoos. A Jungle Party, with auctions and a sit-down dinner, took fundraising to a new level, and became an annual event. Admission fees would soon become another source of revenue.

In 1977, a gorilla named Kamilah was born to Nina and Pete. This was the second gorilla birth at the zoo—Wanto had been born the year before. Baby gorillas and the promise of a new gorilla exhibit helped the public accept the idea of paying to visit the zoo. Admission booths were built, and in June the zoo started charging $1.50 for adults and $.50 for seniors, teens, and children. A Friends of the Zoo group was formed to promote yearly pass sales at $5.00 for an individual and $10.00 for a family. Charging admission did more than raise money. Juvenile vandalism and rowdiness were dramatically reduced because now there was usually an adult with every group of visitors. And the fence that Gus Knudson had wanted finally encircled the zoo.

Nina and Kamilah.

Conserving energy and minimizing the zoo's use of vehicles went hand in hand with the concept of naturalizing the zoo. A pair of Belgian draft horses were first hitched to a wagon on January 4, 1978, and one week later, at least 10 zoo units had their commissary orders delivered by horse and wagon, probably for the first time in at least 50 years. The draft horses, Dick and Dan, soon became great favorites with both zoo staff and visitors. They weighed about 2,100 pounds each and had been bred to pull and carry heavy loads.

Other animals were in the news that year. In January, a female polar bear and her cub were found dead in their bear grotto maternity den. A metal door had been lowered, shutting off the usual air supply, and backup ventilation scuppers were clogged with straw. The bears probably suffocated from lack of oxygen as they slept. No one ever admitted to lowering the door, and the probability that the bears did it themselves seemed remote. Only keepers and construction workers would normally have had access to this behind-the-scenes area. The mystery was never solved, and the staff was suspicious and uneasy for some time to come.

Canid Comings and Goings

· · · · · · ·

On April 16, 1978, six wolves left their exhibit through a hole they made with their teeth by twisting and breaking the steel-mesh fence bordering their enclosure. The wolves had been marking the fence line with urine, and this could have accelerated the weathering of certain fence sections. After the escape, some of the wolves tried to dig their way back into the exhibit but failed because intact sections of the fence plunged 30 inches underground.

After escaping from the wolf enclosure, a young female found a gap under the zoo's perimeter fence and slithered through to the outside world. She led keepers and curator of mammals Lee Werle on a zigzag chase over Phinney Ridge and down the hill to Ballard. They were equipped with two-way radios that enabled everyone searching for her to keep in touch.

Werle said, "I finally caught up with her heading north on 15th Avenue Northwest. She was loping at a fast pace, probably 15 miles per hour. Of course, we were concerned that she might be hit by a car, and a keeper drove his vehicle alongside her while I tried to stay on her tail without causing her to run any faster. Initially, we tried to herd her back towards the zoo but, even though we were able to turn her from the main arterial, she kept on swerving and turning north. I realized that we were getting closer and closer to Carkeek Park, where dense vegetation would make tracking her down and anesthetizing her extremely difficult, which was a major concern." All of the wolves were rounded up and returned to the zoo.

This incident brought public attention to the zoo's inadequate perimeter fence. While funding was available for new construction, the zoo did not have funding for anything other than piecemeal and remedial repairs of the fence line.

On May 18, a University of Washington student spotted four dogs when she arrived to make behavioral observations of the sika deer for a research project. The dogs had either dug under the zoo's fence or found weak spots that allowed them to get into the zoo. Zoo personnel failed to catch the dogs, which had scattered in all directions. All 16 deer were injured, primarily from crashing into the enclosure fence as they were being chased. Three of the deer died from their injuries.

Two days later, dogs got into the zoo again but were chased off by alert keepers. The zoo staff was armed with tranquilizer rifles, and the maintenance staff poured asphalt at the base of perimeter gates and placed several tons of rocks along the fences, but the dogs were back on May 23. This time they attacked six mouflon sheep; a ewe and a lamb died. Curator of education Helen Freeman speculated that the dogs weren't as interested in eating the animals as they were in the thrill of the chase. (*Seattle Times,* May 23, 1978)

Zoo staff had been surveying the fence line for weaknesses immediately after the first incident, but the dogs were still digging under weak portions. Animal control officers were rounding up unleashed dogs in neighborhoods around the zoo, and two keepers were patrolling the zoo all night long. A retired Czechoslovakian forester who specialized in trapping animals suggested that the zoo start baiting traps with cooked liver, but the dogs weren't interested.

After more than a week had passed since the first dog attack, curator of reptiles Ernie Wagner reported that he and another zoo employee had spotted five dogs roaming the grounds at different times. They caught two of them and also found a previously unnoticed hole in the fence. Despite all the publicity, people in the neighborhood were still allowing their dogs to run loose.

On June 13, the Mayor and City Council finally authorized $39,000 for fence repair. By that time, animal control officers had picked up 15 unlicensed dogs in the Woodland Park area and issued 23 citations.

For keepers and other staff, who become emotionally attached to the animals, these deaths were especially disheartening.

Over the years, the zoo had embraced various organizing principles to build collections. At one time, Gus Knudson was interested in showing animals from every state in the union. Ed Johnson, his successor, wanted the collection to be as comprehensive as possible and brought in many animal species that no one in Seattle had ever seen before. Frank Vincenzi also wanted to bring in new species, especially those about which little was known or that were threatened with extinction. Now, the zoo would be displaying animals in mixed groups, based on natural ecosystems.

In 1979, the zoo received its first red pandas, and in preparation for the African Savanna, a one-year-old hippo named Waterlily was transported to Seattle from her birthplace—the Houston Zoo. Lions were given access to an enlarged area that would become part of the savanna exhibit zone.

For several days, the lions did not venture beyond the former boundary of their old outdoor enclosure. Gradually, they ventured farther, exploring their entire space, which had been planted with tall grasses on irregular terrain punctuated by rocky outcrops and

Some traditional zoo professionals and early visitors were taken aback by the sight of unmowed grass at the zoo.

Woodland Park Zoo's lion exhibit. Designers used portions of the old grottos and Feline House to create a naturalistic exhibit for lions in 1979.

shaded by a scattering of trees that closely resembled African acacias. Eventually, the lions would occasionally catch and eat unsuspecting waterfowl that landed in their open exhibit and even catch fish stocked in the bordering stream (water moat). Their predatory instincts were still very much intact.

Monkey Island re-emerged as a naturalistic landscape with waterfalls and lush vegetation. Visitors no longer surrounded the primates. Instead, they were themselves surrounded by a newly planted landscape with nonhuman primates leaping among the branches of living trees.

The Marsh and Swamp also opened in 1979. The words in this exhibit's name were later reversed to "Swamp and Marsh" because many visitors were asking for directions to the "*Martian* Swamp," expecting, perhaps, to find extraterrestrial fauna on display. Later it was called the Wetlands exhibit, tying it in to school curricula and to conservation initiatives that used the term "wetlands."

The zoo world was most interested in the gorilla exhibit. It would be the first naturalistic exhibit for gorillas in the world. When Hancocks had shown plans for the exhibit at a national conference of zoo professionals, he was told that it would never work.

Passages: Frank Vincenzi and Wayne Williams

· · · · · · ·

Former zoo director Frank Vincenzi died in November 1978 at the age of 66, just two years after he had retired. He had worked longer for Seattle's Department of Parks and Recreation than any other employee. When he retired, the dedicated public servant said his greatest regret was that he "couldn't have done more to improve the animals' well-being here."

Former director Frank Vincenzi.

Longtime keeper Wayne Williams with hippo.

That same year, on April 18, 62-year-old senior keeper Wayne Williams died unexpectedly while still on the job. He had been at the zoo since 1962. Williams, who had worked in rodeos, was admired for his understanding of animal behavior and his often fearless ability to work with bears, elephants, otters, camels, and hippos.

Curator of mammals Lee Werle said in 2010, "Wayne had a remarkable way with animals, although most of his hands-on techniques are no longer used. I remember when he worked with about five young black bears that seemed to have imprinted on him. One day, he invited me in to see his 'kids,' and before I knew it, I was sharing a rather small space with five bears while Wayne and I fed them some treats. One of the bears stood upright on its hind legs and Wayne just stomped gently on one of its hind paws and said, 'No!' The bear immediately dropped down on all fours without any visible fear or aggression."

Gorillas were afraid of running water and would never cross the stream that would flow through the landscape; baby gorillas might fall into the stream and drown. Gorillas would eat dirt and get sick, and destroy everything that grows. They might fall out of trees or catch diseases.

The zoo's veterinarian, Jim Foster, however, felt that the potential physical and psychological benefits to the gorillas far outweighed the risks. The zoo's gorillas needed something better than the aging Great Ape House.

CHAPTER ELEVEN

GORILLAS, A SAVANNA, AND A SURPRISE GIFT

THE FIRST OF THE MAJOR NATURALISTIC EXHIBITS opened in 1979. Modeled after gorilla habitat in Equatorial Guinea, it had been designed with input from gorilla researchers George Schaller and Dian Fossey.

Photographs of the completed exhibit were sent to Fossey. She reported that her staff thought the photos were taken in the Virunga Mountains rain forest, and later said in public presentations that Woodland Park Zoo was the only zoo in the world that she considered suitable for captive gorillas.

To prevent gorillas from yanking shrubbery and trees out by the roots, vegetation was given a full year to establish itself. Experienced local mountaineers had scaled the rocky, sculpted-concrete cliff, and the exhibit was then escape-proofed by removing the handholds the human primates had discovered.

For several days before they moved in, the gorillas were allowed to view their new landscape through

LEFT: In 1979, the new gorilla exhibit was the beginning of a brand-new approach.

ABOVE: Kiki up a tree.

doorway grilles. When the doors were finally opened, only a few people already familiar to the gorillas were present, to reduce stress and anxiety. Kiki, the 450-pound dominant male, was the first to venture in. He entered nervously, and seemed intimidated by grass and a crow flying overhead, but soon moved farther into the exhibit, plucked some grass, and tasted some leaves.

Within a week, all of the gorillas had settled into their new exhibit. As predicted, they did uproot many of the plants, but keepers replanted them at night until the novelty of uprooting vegetation wore off. Kiki was fond of climbing a tree that gave him a wide view of the exhibit and the areas beyond it. He would occasionally toss leaves and twigs to other members of the troop below. Despite dire predictions, none of the gorillas were injured by falls.

The Gorilla on the Sidewalk

One day, two visitors walked into the zoo administration building to report that a gorilla was out in a public area. Similar reports had been received before, because the exhibit was designed to create just this kind of illusion. The visitors got the usual reassuring explanation, but as they left the office, one of them was overheard saying, "Still, it just doesn't seem right having him sit there on the sidewalk like that."

Radio calls went out to zoo staff, in a prearranged code used to prevent the public from panicking in case of escapes. The police were called to make sure that crowds could be controlled and that the zoo could be evacuated. When Warren Iliff, then director of Washington Park Zoo in Portland, made an unannounced visit to the zoo specifically to check out the new gorilla exhibit, he was told at the entrance booth that the zoo was temporarily closed. "What's up," he joked. "Did the gorillas get out?"

Some zoos had a "shoot on sight" policy at this time, but Woodland Park did not. It did have emergency procedures in place. The maintenance staff was the first to spot Kiki as he sat on a mound watching polar bears. His location was relayed to veterinarian Jim Foster. Foster and two keepers approached slowly. Kiki recognized Foster and started to follow him back toward the exhibit. Then, Kiki stopped. Foster ordered a bucket of bananas and sliced apples, and Kiki began to follow him again. They finally reached the back of the Nocturnal House, near Kiki's suspected escape route, but

Kiki liked the new exhibit, and soon tested its limits.

Kiki was showing signs of agitation. Foster sat down and offered him some fruit, and the two had a picnic together.

Then Foster led Kiki to an aluminum ladder that had been placed to allow re-entry to the exhibit through a dry moat. Foster climbed down the ladder, hoping that Kiki would follow. Kiki refused. Instead, Kiki began exploring, eventually entering the hallway into the Nocturnal House service area. As Kiki moved through the hallway, Foster slipped in behind him.

Every day, keepers scattered and hid fruit, sunflower seeds, and other food in the landscape before letting the gorillas into the exhibit, so they could forage as they would have in the wild. Keepers were baffled when they noticed that when Kiki was let outside, he went directly to where they had hidden his favorite food. Video cameras in the keepers' office surveyed the outdoor enclosure. From his indoor den, Kiki

Hidden moats and barriers kept carnivores away from their prey in the African Savanna.

had found an angle from which he could watch the monitor, and see the keepers hiding snacks.

The African Savanna opened in July 1980. Many different species shared the same ground plane, including zebras, giraffes, springboks, Kori bustards, crowned cranes, and secretary birds. From certain viewpoints, it appeared as though patas monkeys, lions, and hippos also occupied the same grassy plain. This was accomplished primarily through raised ground planes and the use of hidden moats as barriers. Later, the National Geographic Society accidentally selected a photograph of the patas monkey exhibit for a book on Africa because it looked so realistic that they assumed the photo had been taken in the wild.

Most members of the public agreed that the animals looked more magnificent and dignified than ever before, but some visitors and zoo professionals complained that the animals were too far away. Others assumed that the grass wasn't mowed because maintenance standards had slipped.

The African Savanna resulted in a best new exhibit award presented by the American Association of Zoological Parks and Aquariums (AAZPA) in 1981,

Then Kiki randomly picked a door and turned the handle. The door was locked, but Kiki pulled harder and snapped the lock. He made his way into the Nocturnal House kitchen, where food for various animals was laid out in neatly spaced metal pans. Kiki stepped up onto the table and sampled the food, picking out his favorites—papaya and blueberries.

Meanwhile, Foster prepared a tranquilizer gun, hoping to dart Kiki during a moment of distraction. He didn't want Kiki to associate him with the sting of the dart because this could affect Kiki's willingness to cooperate with him during future health exams or other veterinary procedures. Foster tossed a banana, and as Kiki turned to retrieve it, the dart was fired. Kiki was initially agitated but gradually backed into a corner of the kitchen and lost consciousness. He was carried back to his exhibit on a stretcher.

It appeared that Kiki had uprooted a hawthorn tree that was about six inches in diameter and used it as a ladder to slip to the bottom of the dry moat. Once at the bottom, he merely had to reposition the branch on the other side of the moat to climb up and out.

Gorilla keeper Violet Sunde said that after Kiki recovered from the anesthesia, he lowered himself over the edge of the moat several times and appeared to search for a branch large enough to support his weight as he climbed out. To discourage further escape attempts, an electrified wire was placed along the inside edge of the moat wall. Kiki closely examined it, touched it once, and never went near it again.

Zebras browse among autumn leaves as species from a temperate climate fill in for the vegetation of the African Savanna.

and Tacoma's Point Defiance Zoo was the first to build exhibits in a similar style, hiring designers Jones & Jones. Generally, however, most senior zoo managers and curators thought naturalistic exhibits looked untidy, didn't like allowing animals to disappear from view or restricting public viewing areas to controlled perspectives, and disapproved of dedicating so much space to vegetation.

The innovative exhibits began to attract attention from academia. Scholars and others who had questioned the value of zoos, or felt they should be abolished, came to take a look. The zoo began to draw more highly educated job applicants, attracted by its progressive exhibits and commitment to animal well-being. The number of applicants for a zoo job in the 1960s had averaged about 20; now it was as high as 500 and included applicants from across the nation. The workforce was also changing. The zoo-keeping staff was no longer all-white and all-male.

African Savanna logo designed by Keith Yoshida and Jim Hayes.

New exhibits such as those for gorillas, lions, and Asian primates—initially, lion-tailed macaques—met with the approval of people who had previously complained about inhumane conditions. In 1980, the zoo received a "Top Rating" from the U.S. Humane Society. Only a few other zoos had a "Top Rating" at this time. These included San Diego, Bronx, and Arizona-Sonora Desert Museum. Woodland Park Zoo was the only zoo to move straight from the bottom to the top of the Humane Society's ranking.

As flora met fauna, visitors felt that the natural surroundings gave the animals a new air of dignity and enhanced their natural beauty.

In 1980, Mayor Royer's office called the zoo and eagerly told them that Thai Airways wanted to donate a one-year-old female elephant named Chai to celebrate its purchase of a locally built Boeing 747 airplane. An elephant exhibit was not part of the long-range plan, and Hancocks later wrote, "I believed the public view would eventually come to support the idea of moving the elephants to a better home." (*Crosscut*, April 15, 2015)

But the zoo had a long history of exhibiting elephants, and the community had a long history of giving them to the zoo as gifts. They were also associated with making children happy. When Hancocks balked

at the gift, he received angry phone calls from mothers who wanted their children to be able to see elephants at the zoo, and "gaily colored hate mail" from school-children, written, he assumed, under the direction of their teachers.

He also said that a City Council member asked him how a zoo without an elephant could call itself a zoo, and Hancocks later wrote that he was told that if he raised the question again, "it would be Hancocks leaving Seattle, not the elephants." Hancocks was firmly overruled. He hoped to see a time when Woodland Park's elephants would find a home in a warmer climate and with more space, but that time never came while Hancocks was director. Chai was joined the following year by another one-year-old Asian elephant, named Sri, a gift from a Thai zoo.

Along with elephants, amusement rides also had been a strong tradition at the zoo. Although many people felt nostalgic about the rides and the miniature train they had enjoyed as children, in 1980 these

Lion-tailed macaques grooming on a branch.

The special appeal elephants have for children never wavered over the decades. In the 1980s, young visitors meet a young Chai.

were removed. Designer Grant Jones of Jones & Jones explained that they had to go because they would disrupt the pristine views of the African Savanna, writing that "thousands of hours were spent analyzing views, calculating floor levels, eye levels, and roof levels to ensure most structures would not be visible and that cross-views of other people would be difficult, if not impossible."

There were also philosophical reasons for their removal. The new design had as its goal an environ-ment that promoted both respect for animals and a sense of wonder. Hancocks and the Jones & Jones designers believed that presenting animals near rides suggested that the animals were also there for amuse-ment, serving as curiosity objects or even sideshow freaks. Removing rides for children was also part of a repudiation of the idea that zoos should be designed in large measure for the amusement of children. Similarly, the term "Children's Zoo" was replaced with "Family Farm." Zoos were for people of all ages and meant to be enjoyable, educational, and inspiring with or without the company of children.

"Incompatible Paraphernalia"—Clearing Out the Clutter

The memorial to President Warren G. Harding, who died soon after visiting Woodland Park, ended up buried beneath the African Savanna.

Over the years, various monuments had become part of the zoo, but the focus of the zoo's 1976 master plan was on animals and natural environments. Monuments, characterized as "incompatible paraphernalia" by zoo designer Grant Jones in 1980, were slated for removal.

It would have been hard to argue that the bandstand erected in 1925 to commemorate the 1923 visit to Woodland Park by President Warren G. Harding would make any sense in the African Savanna. Harding had made his last public speech in the park before his death in San Francisco shortly afterward. The Warren G. Harding Lodge of Poulsbo, Washington, who had named their lodge after their brother Mason two days after his death, was contacted about possibly moving the memorial itself, but declined the gift.

Plaques and bronze statues of saluting Boy Scouts that had been part of the memorial were given to Seattle Scout headquarters. When the African Savanna was under construction, a large hole was dug next to the bandstand and the entire structure was tipped into the hole and buried. While visitors can no longer see the frieze by sculptor Alice Robertson Carr de

Creeft, another of her works remains above ground in the Woodland Park Rose Garden.

An old steam locomotive, Great Northern engine #1246, was also removed and sold to a railway buff who intended to restore it. However, it ended up partially disassembled, in a field in southwestern Oregon.

Totem poles had been a cultural icon in Seattle since the 1890s, and in 1939, two of them sprouted on zoo grounds. A Daughters of the American Revolution chapter installed a 16-foot totem pole, carved by Chief William Shelton, in the northern section of the park overlooking Green Lake. The gift celebrated the 50th anniversary of Washington statehood. It was accepted on behalf of the City by Mayor Arthur B. Langlie, with the widow of Chief Shelton and several relatives dressed in traditional white doeskin clothing also in attendance. The totem pole was removed in 1977 for repairs, and never replaced.

The other totem pole was designed by then keeper Frank Vincenzi and carved by WPA laborers. It included the seals of the State of Washington and the City of Seattle, a rhododendron, and various Washington state fauna—salmon, mallard duck, harbor seal, and cougar—as well as the words "Welcome to Woodland Park Zoological Gardens, 1939."

Great Northern steam locomotive in Woodland Park Zoo, circa 1960s. Engine #1246 was later removed after being sold to a railway enthusiast.

GORILLAS, A SAVANNA, AND A SURPRISE GIFT · 107

A totem pole carved by Chief William Shelton was placed at the zoo in 1939.

Some monuments survived because of their location. In 1911, cannons from Spanish-American War hero Admiral Dewey's USS *Concord* were placed in the southwest corner of the zoo, now called the War Memorial Garden. Later additions were a pair of Civil War artillery pieces; "The Hiker," a statue of a Spanish-American War infantryman; and a plaque made of metal from the USS *Maine,* which had exploded and sunk in Havana Harbor in 1898. When a fence was installed later, these items ended up between the fence and the street.

Similarly, the formal rose garden, built on park land set aside for the purpose in 1922, and embellished with a fountain, was separated from the zoo itself and continued as a separate entity outside the gates.

In the years after the monument roundup, items began to find their way back onto zoo grounds, including a Jimi Hendrix memorial and a baby elephant statue. By 1989, the city's One Percent for Art program had become a thorn in the zoo's side. The Arts Commission said it would allow only nontraditional and socially challenging artworks approved by delegates of the Arts Commission and not by the zoo or its designers. The zoo said it preferred art that also emphasized animal forms of realistic scale within a naturalistic landscape, but the commission prevailed.

A less traditional totem pole, designed by Frank Vincenzi, was also created in 1939 and placed in a fallow deer exhibit yard.

CHAPTER TWELVE

HANCOCKS LEAVES,
TOWNE TAKES OVER,
THE COMMUNITY STEPS UP

THE ZOO'S NEW LOOK required a new approach to the plants as well as the animals. There's a difference between naturalistic and natural, and maintaining the new landscape wasn't simply a matter of letting nature take its course. While there was less mowing and weeding flower beds, there was more soil preparation, naturalistic pruning, and replacing plants destroyed by animals. In 1982, Sue Maloney Nicol became the first horticulturist assigned specifically to the zoo. During the next 16 years, she participated on the planning and design teams for all new exhibits, spearheaded the national recognition of zoo horticulture as an integral part of zoo operations, and served as president of the Association of Zoological Horticulture in 1986.

In 1982, after a period of dramatic relandscaping, smaller projects were under way. The Backyard Ecology exhibit focused on plants for local wildlife, partially funded by the Seattle Audubon Society and

ABOVE: Sue Maloney Nicol helped bring zoo horticulture to the forefront and raise awareness of the importance of zoo flora for animals and visitors alike.

LEFT: Hippos have long been important zoo residents. Their living environments have evolved multiple times over the years.

the Burlington Northern Railroad. The giraffes were moved to the African Savanna, and their barn was refitted for a kangaroo exhibit almost entirely by volunteers. A snow leopard exhibit under construction was of particular interest to attendees at the Third International Snow Leopard Symposium, hosted by the zoo that year.

After the excitement of the zoo's major overhaul, things were slowing down. Attendance at the zoo during 1982 was down, no major exhibits had opened that year, the local economy was suffering, and regional tourism was down. But the zoo hadn't been forgotten. A *Seattle Times* editorial read, "In a time of economic recession and widespread unemployment, some may think it more appropriate to give money to programs that help people, not animals. But the way we treat the other inhabitants of our planet—especially endangered species—is an important part of our 'humanity,' too. And for many animals, zoos are now the last stop between survival and extinction." (John Hamer, *Seattle Times*, Dec. 9, 1982)

By the end of the year, the zoo's first ever mass-media campaign was under way. Advertising agency

Note a wild Canada goose spotted from a viewpoint of the African Savanna. A nearby hippo ignores it, but resident lions occasionally kill and consume wild birds landing in their exhibit.

Zoo animals were seen all over town on Metro buses during the 1982 mass-media campaign.

Chiat/Day/Livingston donated about $30,000 in staff time. Media Networks Inc. contributed magazine ads, and Ackerley Communications, Inc., provided billboards at reduced cost.

In 1982 the Seattle Zoological Society worked with KEZX radio and the Seattle Foundation to raise funds for a much-needed renovation of the Pheasantry, later called the Conservation Aviary. In 1983 the zoo partnered again with the head of KEZX, David Littrell, on a concert series. Musicians performed in the Parks Department's "show mobile," parked in the North Meadow. The concerts gave the zoo a new way to serve the public and raise money. Through many sound tests, keepers and other employees worked together to make sure that volume levels wouldn't disturb the animals and that sound was projected away from the more sensitive animals. The concert series evolved into a 33-year-old summer tradition—ZooTunes—featuring rock, folk, soul, and blues acts. This series regularly attracts sell-out crowds of over 3,000 people.

In 1982 two new overlooks were created at the African Savanna—one at the hippo exhibit and another at the south end of the Savanna. A viewpoint at this location had been part of the Savanna design, but there wasn't enough funding to build it before the Savanna opened.

When radio station KZOK started a fundraising campaign for a Jimi Hendrix memorial at the zoo, Hancocks saw an opportunity to fund the viewpoint while simultaneously accommodating the community's desire to honor the Seattle native. The whole idea was controversial. KZOK had neglected to let the Parks Department know about its campaign before it was launched. Department policy said memorials couldn't be placed in parks. The zoo had already cleared out the Harding memorial and a steam engine a few years before. There was also opposition because of Hendrix's connection with drugs, and some felt that honoring an African American musician in a zoo had racist overtones.

Eventually, Superintendent of Parks Walt Hundley and Seattle's Board of Park Commissioners approved the memorial. Purple and orange tiles with swirling flames were placed on the walkway, and purple-leaved barberry shrubs were planted nearby to evoke Hendrix's composition "Purple Haze." The broader design for the viewpoint was inspired by another Hendrix song, "Third Stone from the Sun." A brass sunburst on one of the artificial rocks at the new viewpoint bore an inscription dedicating the overlook to his memory. The inscribed rock is also what exhibit technicians

After the zoo cleared out two memorials, a new one, honoring local musician Jimi Hendrix, was installed in 1983.

refer to as a "hot rock." It includes a heating coil that can be turned on during cold weather. Hot rocks are used in some exhibits so cold animals can choose warmer microclimates. Jimi Hendrix's father, Al, unveiled the memorial on Thursday, June 9, 1983.

It was arguably a stretch to explain the reasoning behind the memorial and its placement—a project that began as a radio station promotion—but Hancocks managed to come up with some rather convoluted prose to put it all in some sort of context: "I hope the contemplative nature of the memorial . . . and its location as a stage in front of the Savanna wildlife will encourage people to reflect upon the connections between Hendrix's upbringing in Seattle, his roots in Africa, his music in the United States, and his premature death in England. I hope the new viewpoint might help many to see a new point of view."

In the early 1980s, funding became a challenge and the elephants still needed a better home than their old barn.

By the beginning of 1983, the zoo's portion of the 1968 bond issue—$4.5 million—was gone, and the nation's economy was in a slump. Funding for public works projects, including zoo improvements, had dried up. The zoo was still a patchwork of the old and new. Most of the monkeys were still housed in the 70-year-old Primate House. The Aviary was rotting away, and the zoo's four elephants lived in a barn that was much the same as when Tusko and Wide Awake were in residence.

Parks administrators saw the zoo as a way to gain support for a bond issue that bundled zoo improvements with other items on their wish list, such as drainage systems for ball fields and new roofing for indoor pools in parks around the city. Voters rejected it. After eight years on the job, Hancocks turned in his resignation in December 1983, and left the zoo in April 1984. Hancocks wrote, "I wore myself out trying to get some of the funding problems solved at Woodland Park." (David Hancocks, Special to the Times, *Seattle Times*, April 1, 1984)

In 1986, Hancocks moved to Australia to complete a master plan for the Melbourne Zoo and prepare a concept plan for Melbourne's gorilla exhibit. He later worked on projects for the Singapore Zoo, served as director of the Arizona-Sonora Desert Museum, wrote a book about his views on zoos, *A Different Nature*, and returned to Australia to serve as director of Victoria's Open Range Zoo.

Hancocks' high-profile departure and the juxtaposition of old, obsolete exhibitry with newer exhibits sparked the formation of a fundraising committee for the zoo initiated by a young lawyer, Richard (Dick) Swanson, and business leaders Bob Davidson and Gerry Johnson. They had seen animals move into spacious surroundings that really did resemble their natural habitats, and walk on grass or climb trees beneath an open sky for the first time in their lives.

On February 17, 1984, they wrote a letter to Mayor Royer with copies sent to four community leaders, including a call to action and a sense of urgency. "Timing is critical. We believe there is now a unique opportunity to take advantage of this public attention by charting a course of action to complete the zoo renovation." This inspired a new direction for the zoo over the next decade.

After a national search and a competitive selection process, David L. Towne, the only local candidate in a field of six, was hired as zoo director. Dave Towne

C. David Hughbanks, president of the Zoo Society, Virgil Fassio, chair of Save Our Elephants, and David Williams, Rainier Bank, at the opening of the new elephant exhibit.

was born in Winslow, Washington, in 1931. After he graduated from Renton High School, he earned a business administration degree at the University of Washington, and went on to a career in public service.

Growing up, he had spent five years on farms in Auburn, south of Seattle, and said that this interlude was the longest continuous association with animals he had before coming to work at the zoo. But Towne had been Superintendent of Seattle's Department of Parks and Recreation from 1973 to 1977, and he understood the City's policies and procedures as well as its politics. He then worked for seven years in the private sector, primarily with landscape architects Jones & Jones and Coffman Engineers in Bellevue, firms that were working with zoos across the country. During his time as superintendent, he'd been in the thick of debates about the Bartholick plan and funding, and he was on record as having said, "A zoo should be done right or not at all."

He was also involved in the development of the Seattle Aquarium and the creation of the zoo's long-range plan. And as a consultant in the private sector, he had assisted with the planning and implementation of several zoo and aquarium master plans elsewhere in the U.S.

One of the first things he wanted to address was the Elephant House, which despite changing ideas about animal welfare, had not changed much since the days of Wide Awake and Tusko. It was a drafty, unheated bunker—dark, oppressive, and stark.

And another issue was simmering. Animal-rights activists and others were upset to learn that chickens, goats, and sheep who had grown too old or too big for the Family Farm—part of the renamed Children's Zoo—were being used to feed lions and tigers and other carnivores. There was heated debate about the practice in the media, City Hall, and the boardroom of Seattle's Department of Parks and Recreation.

The zoo had used some of its own animals to feed carnivores since its inception. Many people thought it was only rational that the same farm animals that humans eat would be used to feed felines and other carnivores. They would be eating slaughtered animals from other sources in any case. But the critics felt strongly that the zoo animals should be allowed to live out their natural lives.

Carnivore Catering

From the beginning, the zoo took feeding its animals seriously. Under Gus Knudson, apprentice keepers were required to study the natural food of animals and pass a test to become junior feeders, eventually becoming senior feeders after they had acquired more knowledge. In a newspaper article, Knudson explained that "all of our specimens must have proper vitamins." He added, "And nearly all get cod liver oil."

In its early days, the zoo bought geriatric or lame horses from an individual who traveled the state buying them up, and also accepted old horses as donations. Keepers had to kill and butcher the horses before feeding them to the zoo's carnivores. Although horsemeat was important to the zoo for more than 60 years, other livestock species were also used, and many of these, such as rabbits, were raised at the

Feeding carnivores whole or sectioned carcasses gives them the natural stimulation they experience in the wild.

zoo, either at the Family Farm or the commissary where food for all the animals was processed. As a keeper, Frank Vincenzi prepared trays of rats, mice, and eggs for carnivorous reptiles; rats and mice were hunted in the zoo buildings they infested.

Former curator of mammals Lee Werle remembered the day when he was a keeper feeding rabbits to carnivores in the Feline House. Part of his job was to club a rabbit and toss it through a feeding chute in a tiger's holding den. After placing a rabbit through the feeding chute—something he had done many times before—he went about the rest of his duties in the Feline House. A little later, he heard an eerie, low-pitched wail coming from somewhere in the holding area. Werle quickly walked along the row of dens to investigate, and realized that the unusual sound was coming from the tiger he had just given the rabbit to. The tiger was standing almost upright on its hind legs, clawing at the top of the den wall as though trying to climb it—all the while wailing in distress. The tiger's meal had suddenly come to life and was hopping around in the tiger den. The tiger had never seen a live rabbit before, and Werle had never seen such a terrified tiger. Werle let the cat out into the exhibit, then went into the den and made sure the rabbit would be motionless when the tiger came back in.

While zoos don't generally feed live prey to carnivores, feeding whole or sectioned carcasses gives carnivores the natural stimulation of plucking feathers from chickens or pulling the fur off a dead rabbit. In the absence of such opportunities, some carnivores may begin to pluck their own fur or feathers. Feeding intact carcasses can enhance the health of an animal by providing certain physical and cognitive stimuli associated with eating in the wild.

Towne didn't want any bad publicity surrounding the surplus farm animals to slow down doing something about the living conditions for the elephants. Farm animals couldn't be given or sold to anyone outside the zoo, including farmers, because of United States Department of Agriculture (USDA) regulations designed to prevent pathogens from exotic species from being passed on to domestic livestock. Other zoos already faced problems of overcrowding and an overabundance of geriatric animals in their domestic species collections, and wouldn't take them. Eventually, the zoo was able to get an exemption from the USDA regulations so that surplus animals from the Family Farm could be given to farmers or others who could care for them properly.

Emergency repairs to the elephant barn were proposed and some were made, but Towne argued that it was important to look beyond a "Band-Aid solution." He asked Jones & Jones to develop a concept for an "Elephant Forest" exhibit that would include not only Asian elephants but also other species native to tropical Asia.

Over the years, city government had sometimes ignored pleas for adequate zoo funding, but now concern about the state of the zoo was hard to ignore. Since implementing the Elephant Forest plan would be expensive, Mayor Charles Royer asked the community to step up. If individuals and corporations could raise half of the $6.7 million needed for design and construction, government would find the other half.

David Williams addresses the opening ceremony of the Elephant Forest exhibit with Mayor Charles Royer and children who raised money for the exhibit.

CHAPTER THIRTEEN

A New Era Begins,
Farewell to Snowflake, and
Adding Humans to Habitat

THE YEAR 1984 MARKED THE BEGINNING of a new era for the zoo. Zoo Society president C. David Hughbanks led development of a new logo designed by Jim Hayes in 1984, created with art direction from Keith Yoshida, who was responsible for graphics design and production at the zoo for more than 20 years. Yoshida asked Hayes to include plants in the logo to represent habitat as well as animals. The logo won design awards, and other zoos began using remarkably similar logos. Towne found himself making firm but friendly calls to other zoos to discuss copyright infringement. The Seattle Zoological Society adopted the zoo's new logo and also changed its name to the Woodland Park Zoological Society.

At the urging of Bill Stafford of the Mayor's Office, *Seattle Post-Intelligencer* publisher Virgil Fassio and Robert Truex and David Williams of Rainier Bank accepted the mayor's invitation to lead the Save Our Elephants fundraising campaign. In November 1984,

the *Post-Intelligencer* donated $60,000 toward the elephant exhibit's design, and King County committed to match the donation—an unprecedented step that reflected the fact that Woodland Park Zoo served not only Seattle residents, but people throughout the region.

Looking beyond the elephants, and at the request of

Zoo Society leaders Dick Swanson, Gerry Johnson, and Bob Davidson, Mayor Royer invited 50 interested citizens from throughout the county to serve on a commission that would make recommendations for both a plan for the

LEFT: East African bush elephant Watoto in autumn leaves, 2009.

ABOVE: The Save Our Elephants campaign launched on November 15, 1984.

future of the zoo and a way to fund the plan. Former State Senator Walt Williams agreed to chair the commission, and he and his family became generous supporters of the zoo.

Williams, Towne, and the commission met almost weekly through the next year to confirm affordable projects and to consult with elected officials and financial advisors. They also conducted polls, which showed that 70 percent of King County residents would be likely to support a bond issue for zoo improvements.

The Zoo Commission delivered its final report on May 8, 1985, and proposed a countywide bond issue to be augmented by funds raised from the private sector. Historian Walt Crowley later called it "an audacious proposal on several counts," because if the bond issue made it onto the ballot, residents outside Seattle would be asked to impose additional taxes on themselves to help build a facility located in the city.

Of equal importance, the Zoo Society would be asked to raise more than $10 million, although it had never raised more than a few hundred thousand dollars. In addition, a minimum of 60 percent of voters would have to vote "yes" for the bond issue to pass.

After extensive negotiations, the city and county officials, led by Mayor Royer, City Council President Norm Rice, and County Executives Tim Hill and Randy Revelle, as well as County Council Chair Lois North, agreed to place the $31.5 million bond issue on the countywide November 1985 ballot. Time was short before the election, and there was confusion about the difference between supporting a new elephant exhibit and the broader zoo bond issue. Eventually, efforts to promote the two issues were merged to create more support for the zoo.

Representatives of the zoo bond committee, Zoo Commission, and Zoo Society worked hard to gain support for the zoo issue among politicians and com-

Dave Towne (right) watches Hank Klein, the zoo's public relations chief, dressed as a gorilla in support for the zoo bond at the Westin Hotel, 1985.

munity leaders. Towne, Swanson, and newly appointed Zoo Society CEO Bob Davidson worked to get support for the bond issue and the zoo in general, pointing to the success of the zoo's radical naturalistic exhibits built in 1979 and 1980, as well as the importance of creating humane exhibits for the animals that were still kept in cages of concrete and steel. The new exhibits were clearly perceived as much better for the physical and psychological health of the animals. Zoo Society president Dick Swanson often said, "The quality of our zoo is a measure of our grace."

During a time of tight municipal budgets, shrinking federal aid, and growing problems such as homelessness, some people felt that human problems should be addressed ahead of any needs at the zoo. Towne brought years of political experience to the job, and worked hard to get support for the bond issue and the zoo in general among politicians and community leaders.

He especially enjoyed bringing them together at the zoo. They could find common ground and forget their differences as they experienced the thrill of feeding a carrot to an elephant and touching its trunk. Visits to the zoo also brought politicians and community leaders face to face with the zoo's multigenerational family audience.

The zoo bond passed with an impressive 71 percent majority. Now, the Zoo Society had to reinvent itself

Towne knew that personal and direct experience with the animals of the zoo was a powerful driver of support.

to raise those matching millions it had committed to add. The Zoo Society had only two employees—and one of them worked part-time. Dick Swanson and many others labored to counter the perception that zoo bonds would take care of everything, when actually a dollar of private funding was needed for the release of every three dollars from bond funding.

In the spring of 1985, with the support of Bill Stafford of the mayor's office, a Woodland Park Zoo delegation composed of Dave Towne, Dick Swanson, Walt Williams, and Dwight Dively traveled to China, and discussed the possibility of exchanges with a zoo there. As a result of their visit, the Zoo Society later hosted a four-member delegation from Chongqing and received a pair of red pandas and several pheasant

species. In exchange, Woodland Park Zoo sent some of its animals to the Chongqing Zoo. Arrangements were also made for a pair of golden monkeys (Hong Hong and Yang Yang) to be exhibited temporarily at Woodland Park Zoo, from February through April of 1986. It was only the second time that golden monkeys had been exhibited in the western world.

Thanks to the generosity of Jim Johnson, vice president of Alaska Airlines and Zoo Society Board

Dave Towne, Irene Cheyne of the Woodland Park Zoo Society, Marcia and Dick Swanson, and Stephanie and Bill Stafford with Bamboo in 1986.

Polar bears had been a part of the Woodland Park Zoo family for a long time. Here China inspects an apple, circa early 1950s.

as exciting as looking at a rug on a stick. They decided to come up with an educational program that could be offered before visitors stepped into the koala viewing area, to prepare them for the potential disappointment of watching a koala sleep. The zoo teamed up with KOMO-TV and local weatherman Steve Pool to develop an educational video on koala conservation that showed on a loop in an alcove near the exhibit. By the time zoo guests reached the viewing area, they fully expected to see a sleeping koala, and if the koala moved at all, they were thrilled. After the koala exhibit closed, napping Nutsy was transported back to San Diego Zoo in a carrier kennel kept in first-class seating on Alaska Airlines. Woodland Park Zoo offered a special tour for docents to accompany the koala and get a behind-the-scenes tour of the San Diego Zoo.

On January 17, 1986, Woodland Park Zoo's last remaining polar bear, Snowflake, who had been born at the zoo in 1964, moved to Tacoma's Point Defiance Zoo & Aquarium, where she could live in a state-of-the-art exhibit. Zoo employees usually experience sadness when they say good-bye to the animals they have cared for.

In 1987, a koala on loan from San Diego arrives on Alaska Airlines with plenty of eucalyptus leaves.

member, another temporary exhibit, featuring a koala on loan from San Diego Zoo, opened in 1987. Alaska Airlines donated transportation from San Diego for Nutsy the koala and her keeper, Valerie Thompson. Alaska Airlines also transported plenty of eucalyptus, the koala's primary food, from growers in southern California.

Koalas are mostly nocturnal and sleep for as long as 20 hours a day. The staff worried that a koala sleeping in a potted tree in the animal nursery would be about

Squirrel Monkeys Scatter

On the Fourth of July, 1987, 20 squirrel monkeys celebrated Independence Day by escaping into the surrounding neighborhood.

On the Fourth of July, 1987, a group of newly acquired young squirrel monkeys were released into the portion of the naturalistic Primate Islands exhibit that used to be called Monkey Island. The zoo introduces animals to an exhibit in much the same way they are released in the wild to bolster diminishing populations. The process includes holding the animals in cages positioned within the new environment where keepers observe them, feed them, give them water, and provide enrichment items—professional zoo jargon for toys given to animals to allow them to mimic the behavior of their species in the wild, or to prevent boredom—until the animals appear to be settled in.

After the novelty of the new surroundings wears off, the cage doors are left open so animals can explore the external environment at will and retreat to the security of their introduction cage at any time. Food is scattered outside the cage to encourage longer exploration times at greater distances. The radius of exploration begins to increase.

When the animals choose to spend more time outside the cages than inside, cages are removed.

When keepers and other employees prepare for exhibit introductions, they always evaluate possible escape routes. They had recently pruned tree branches inside the squirrel monkeys' enclosure to discourage them from trying to leap across the 16-foot water moat. But no one realized that vegetation in the visitor areas had also grown significantly.

When the monkeys were given access to the exhibit, about half of them charged to the ends of willow branches and became airborne, hurling themselves onto vegetation on the visitors' side of the moat. While the new monkeys led the charge, other monkeys soon followed. From there, most of them kept going. Staff members carrying radios and waving long-handled nets sprang into action. The monkeys' radius of exploration extended into surrounding neighborhoods. Of the 20 escapees, some returned to the exhibit on their own, one was killed by a car, and others were lured into transport cages with food. But the count was one monkey short. No one knows what ever happened to the last monkey. Bill Stafford, who had named the Save Our Elephants campaign and later became deputy mayor, said the escape was a true example of celebrating Independence Day.

After any escape, the animal management staff conducts an analysis and develops procedures to prevent future occurrences. The zoo also conducts emergency drills. These practice sessions cover animal escapes and a range of other emergencies including fire, venomous snakebites, and natural disasters such as earthquakes. A darting team is prepared to fire tranquilizers to subdue an animal, and a firearms team is trained to shoot an animal when there are no other alternatives. A review of historical records indicates that Woodland Park Zoo has never had to use the latter option, although there have been rumors that many decades ago, a tiger escaped from the zoo at night and was shot dead on the street without the public ever learning about it.

But when keeper Wendy Wienker and curator of mammals Lee Werle watched Snowflake slip into a saltwater pool at her new home, they felt jubilant. Snowflake's name was changed to Dixie at the Point Defiance Zoo & Aquarium, where she lived until October 18, 1995. She was the last polar bear to have lived at Woodland Park Zoo.

By the end of 1987, the Zoo Society had raised an unprecedented $1.9 million and assumed direct

A new home for the elephants signaled a new exhibit approach using elements of human culture associated with a species.

management of membership programs as well as services such as gift and book sales. The Society presented its first contribution to match bond funds on September 30. Now, the elephants could get their new home.

The Elephant Forest exhibit marked a clear departure from the naturalistic landscapes of the gorilla, savanna, Asian primate, and other exhibits created under the zoo's long-range plan. The design included elements based on human activity.

Because of Seattle's climate, the elephants had to have an indoor heated shelter, and it had to be big.

And to provide office space for keepers, lockers, a shower room, a restroom, and an area for hay storage, the facility would have to be even larger. It wouldn't be possible to screen out the entire building with landscape and still allow visitors to view elephants when the animals were inside.

The design by Johnpaul Jones and Keith Larson of Jones & Jones incorporated a barn that resembled temples in Thailand and replicas of a barrier from the Royal Elephant Stockade, a Thai village based on a cluster of buildings at a Thai historic site, and a replica logging camp. In an effort to create a culturally authentic exhibit, the zoo's education curator had hiked into a remote Thai logging camp and bought items used in the logging industry for display.

Jones & Jones tweaked the ideals of realism and landscape immersion by adding the human element. They divided the 2.6 acres into three zones, with sections dedicated to elephants in the wild, elephants in Thai logging culture, and elephants in Thai religious culture.

Zoo staff members worked with members of the Seattle Thai community to make sure that the details of the exhibit were as authentic as possible and that all cultural interpretation was respectful and accurate. The buildings and the water features were given Thai names.

And the zoo also came up with a name for the new approach. Grant Jones introduced the term "cultural resonance" to the zoo profession in the title of a paper he delivered at the 1989 national conference of the American Association of Zoological Parks and Aquariums (AAZPA). Cultural resonance comes into play when zoo exhibits evoke the presence of people who actually live in or near the animal's natural habitat.

CHAPTER FOURTEEN

STAGECRAFT, HORTICULTURE, A NEW FOREST, AND A NEW JUNGLE

THE ELEPHANT FOREST EXHIBIT opened with great fanfare on June 17, 1989. Vorakron Tantranont, the mayor of Chiang Mai, Thailand, donated several water-storage bowls for display within the Thai Village. During the dedication of the Elephant Forest, Mayor Charles Royer drank water dipped from one of the containers donated by his counterpart in Thailand.

Designer Grant Jones, zoo project manager Jim Maxwell, and elephant keeper Ellen Leach had traveled to Thailand to learn about elephant habitat. The search for authentic environments led the team to a logging camp where elephants were used to haul and stack logs. This had been a traditional use of elephants in Thailand for many generations. Elephants, being good swimmers, were even used to break up logjams in rivers.

While elephant logging in Thailand had ended, logging demonstration programs had been established there, where tourists could watch elephants responding

LEFT: A Tropical Rain Forest exhibit opened in 1992 and featured 86 species, including this hornbill.

to as many as 30 different commands as they performed traditional tasks. The zoo decided to offer a similar program. Before the exhibit opened, the zoo's elephants had been trained to pull, stack, and unstack logs.

A large naturalistic pool fed by a waterfall allowed the elephants to become completely submerged and to

BELOW: Bamboo liked to play with the logs even when not performing with zookeepers.

Elephants had free access to a heated interior. The design of the facility was based on the architecture of temples in Northern Thailand (see inset).

"snorkel" with their trunks for the first time. A sound system was integrated with a seating area so that keepers could provide interpretive commentary to the public as they watched the elephants swimming or wading on their own.

The design of the saddle shed was based on those found in elephant logging camps in the 1980s. The saddle pads and other tack displayed under the roof are from Thailand. The inset photo was taken in Thailand and the larger photo at the zoo's Elephant Forest exhibit.

Before the opening of the elephant exhibit, the zoo was still getting complaints about not keeping the savanna grasses mowed like a lawn. Since the Elephant Forest was adjacent to the Savanna and relatively large, visitors now understood that the zoo was trying to emulate natural habitats.

The Elephant Forest exhibit won awards for the zoo and for Jones & Jones, including the 1990 best exhibit award from the American Association of Zoological Parks and Aquariums (AAZPA). Also, in 1989, Woodland Park Zoo was voted one of the top 10 zoos in the U.S. by a committee of zoo directors and animal-rights organizations.

Interior barrier posts were inspired by those seen at the Royal Elephant Stockade in Thailand.

That same year, a special artificial-insemination procedure was used on white eared-pheasants, one of the species that came to the zoo as a gift from Chongqing, Seattle's sister city in China. This hatching resulted in chicks that were unrelated to most of the other white eared-pheasants in the western world. This was significant because other institutions wanted to diversify their gene pools, as inbreeding had produced a high degree of relatedness among individuals of this species in North American zoos and aviaries.

In 1989, the zoo bred Solomon Island leaf frogs for the first time in captivity, an accomplishment that later generated a Significant Breeding Award from AAZPA. The zoo also received an award from the American Federation of Aviculture for the first captive breeding of gold-whiskered barbets.

In 1991, Bobo and Fifi's old Ape House was demolished to clear ground for the new Tropical Rain Forest exhibit. The orangutans were moved to one of the bear grottos, over which a metal lid had been placed with side panels of heavy wire mesh connected to the enclosure lid. Hammocks and sturdy fire hoses were placed inside the enclosure, and a sign explained that this was a temporary facility for orangutans while their new naturalistic exhibit was being prepared.

Landscape immersion was still the dominant approach in the Elephant Forest exhibit, which was planted in 1988 and 1989.

For the first time, the zoo's elephants could submerge themselves fully in water and even use their trunks as snorkels.

Orangutans eventually settled into a naturalistic exhibit with running water and living plants.

Visitors could look into the forest canopy exhibit, designed for birds.

be tranquilized. Fortunately, the situation was resolved within a few hours.

In 1992, the zoo's last bison was moved to Northwest Trek in Eatonville, Washington. There had been

Schoolchildren were there as tropical butterflies were released into the forest canopy, an indoor portion of the Tropical Rain Forest exhibit.

Less than two weeks after a disaster drill, in which the fictional scenario was that male orangutan Towan had escaped, all five orangutans actually did escape from their temporary grotto exhibit. Keepers tried to lure the orangutans back with treats, but it was clear that they wanted to explore. Next, water was squirted from fire hoses to encourage them to return to their holding area.

The orangutans appeared not to be bothered by the water and chose to stay outside. Some of them picked up the fire hoses and were pointing them back at the keepers—the first human vs. animal water fight recorded at the zoo. Eventually, most of them had to

bison at the zoo since the early 1900s. The bison barn would have to be removed to make way for the Northern Trail exhibit. By this time Northwest Trek had developed considerable expertise with bison, and there was no need to duplicate their efforts at Woodland Park Zoo.

In August, a new $4.8 million Animal Health Complex was completed, and at that time it was considered one of the top five zoo veterinary hospitals in the country. That year also marked the zoo's first attempt to artificially inseminate elephants.

The Tropical Rain Forest exhibit opened to the public on September 15, 1992. Designed by Seattle's Portico Group and Arthur Erickson of Vancouver, B.C., the exhibit covered about 2.5 acres and included more than 800 plant species, 86 animal species, and 20 indoor and five outdoor exhibits.

Birds were to occupy the forest canopy exhibit when it opened, but the animal management staff felt that more time was needed to acclimatize them. The zoo released tropical butterflies in the canopy instead. On opening day, schoolchildren were thrilled to participate in the release of butterflies. Most butterflies have a very short life expectancy as adults, so birds were phased

The Tropical Rain Forest exhibit included more than 800 plant species.

Crested oropendola at the zoo, circa 2007.

into the exhibit as the butterflies approached the end of their lives.

The Tropical Rain Forest incorporated the already existing Gorilla and Asian Primates exhibits and added another gorilla exhibit so that two troops could be kept in separate enclosures.

Some staff members had taken personal vacations to the tropics to acquire firsthand knowledge for the exhibit design. One of them, John Bierlein, photographed rain forest settings at various heights above the forest floor at a remote research station in Costa Rica. He also made rubber acetate and plaster of Paris molds of leaves, wild tropical fruits, seeds, and animal tracks.

Plaster of Paris molds of paca tracks, obtained with the help of children living along the Sarapiquí River in Costa Rica, were used to create impressions on artificial soil banks in the exhibit. Other landscape props included a leafcutter ant trail, matamata turtle bones,

nesting burrows with simulated eggs of the motmot bird, and beetle specimens attached to tree trunks and branches beyond the reach of visitors.

With the help of a professor at the University of Washington, abandoned oropendola bird nests were collected by the staff of the Organization for Tropical Studies. These served as references for artificial nests created by exhibit technician Stephanie Snyder. Shortly after the artificial nests were placed in the exhibit, the crested oropendolas began to build their own nests. This species nests in colonies, and some members of the staff theorized that the presence of other nests might have encouraged the nest-building behavior.

A soundscape including recordings of running water and various animal vocalizations was installed by Muzak, an international company best known for providing "elevator music," and the interior exhibits were arranged in layers to show visitors how certain species spent most of their lives in only one or two layers of a tropical forest. The exhibit had both indoors and outdoors areas. An interior landscape that used both real and artificial plants was the zoo's first attempt to bring the principle of landscape immersion indoors.

In the early 1990s, large areas of the zoo became a construction zone. In 1993 alone, projects under way included the Northern Trail, Family Farm, Temperate Forest, and Trail of Vines. Parts of the Savanna were renovated, a food pavilion site was being prepared, underground utilities were upgraded, and a new education center was being built.

New routes changed almost daily. Zoo-goers could visit interpretive "job shacks" at several locations, look at plans and drawings, and even put on a hard hat. A viewing shelter near the Northern Trail project housed an elaborate 3-D model of the exhibit.

There were some big changes ahead.

Horticulture and Stagecraft Come Together

· · · · · · ·

By this time, Woodland Park Zoo had one of the more notable botanical collections in the Pacific Northwest. With 23 species of bamboo in the Elephant Forest, the zoo already hosted the largest publicly accessible bamboo collection in the Pacific Northwest. With the addition of 30 species of palms in the Tropical Rain Forest, it now offered the most extensive palm collection north of San Francisco. When the exhibit opened, it contained 1,000 orchids of 90 species, and many orchid enthusiasts came to the zoo just to see them.

Planting of new exhibits had been brought in-house by this time, directed by zoo horticulturist Sue Maloney Nicol. The zoo's horticulture staff was careful not to overuse familiar tropical houseplants or to stage showy flowers in large groups. The zoo's horticulturists took "nature as the norm" and attempted to represent tropical rain forest vegetation as authentically as possible. The goal was to pay tribute to the diversity of tropical species and to demonstrate that species are widely scattered in tropical forests. Unlike plants in temperate forests, tropical plants rarely grow in large groups of the same species.

Live vegetation within the building was augmented by artificial trees with embedded planters, simulated vines, and even artificial fruits. The scale and detail of artificial exhibitry in the Tropical Rain Forest exhibit went far beyond anything that Woodland Park Zoo had done up to this point, and it won the top exhibit award presented at AAZPA's national conference the following year.

During the 1980s, the zoo staff wanted to make improvements to smaller exhibits. They were worried that bond funds could only be used for the major projects identified in the ballot measure. In 1987, they had hired a zoo exhibit technician, Stephanie Snyder. She had a background in fine arts and materials science, and had already improved several exhibits at the Seattle Aquarium as well as the zoo.

Zoo staff members were also excited about the interpretive and scenic potential of artificial exhibitry. If these functions could be assumed by the zoo rather than contracted out, the zoo would have more direct control of the work, and it might ultimately be less expensive. Towne decided to initiate a small in-house exhibits team, and a supervisor of exhibits position was approved in the zoo's budget. Larry Sammons, who had worked on the Tropical Rain Forest and had an extensive background in theatrical set design, was hired to fill this position in June 1992.

Many of Sammons' team members had worked as exhibit technicians or grips at the Seattle Opera and theaters at Seattle Center. The exhibits team grew considerably during the decade that followed. They improved many older exhibits and built some of the zoo's smaller exhibits in their entirety. By the end of 1992, the perspectives of theatrical set design and landscape design were both represented by employees at Woodland Park Zoo. They dramatically influenced many new exhibits built during the years ahead.

By the 1990s, Woodland Park Zoo had become a showcase for botany as well as zoology.

CHAPTER FIFTEEN

A Building Boom and the "Best Year Ever"

DAVE TOWNE CALLED 1994 "the zoo's best year ever." More than 16 acres of new facilities and exhibits were opened. A new south entry plaza was completed next to the new ZooStore. Native species and a chain of boulders were part of the plaza. The staff called it an "energy absorbing" landscape because while adults stood in line, children scampered among the trees and hopped on boulders.

In April 1994, a 10-acre Discovery Loop was unveiled, including the new Temperate Forest, Family Farm, and Habitat Discovery area, and retaining the Wetlands exhibit, previously known as the Swamp and Marsh exhibit, and the Pheasantry. The Temperate Forest section included animals from some of Seattle's sister cities, including elegant red-crowned cranes from Kobe, Japan. In the Contact Area, where visitors could interact with uncaged animals, asphalt was replaced by animal-friendly surfaces. Trees were added to give

domestic animals more shade and shelter and allow them to browse. A butterfly garden included information for gardeners on native butterfly species and the plants that attract them.

The zoo had a new landscape policy for this area. As ornamentals died, they would be replaced by native species. Some upright snags were created for use by native urban wildlife, including cavity nesters such as black-capped chickadees and flickers.

The area instantly became a popular play space. Children whose parents remembered Kiddyland and the miniature train were given an environment designed for learning through engaging experiences, such as climbing a giant spider web. A sign at the beginning of the Habitat Discovery Loop included a quotation attributed to educator Jean Piaget: "Activity is indispensable to learning, thinking, and knowing."

The Rain Forest Café, later renamed the Rain Forest Food Pavilion, was a new year-round restaurant that was also a banquet facility. The opening of the Seattle Rotary Education Center, with classrooms and

LEFT: Launched in 1994, the Northern Trail exhibit featured panoramic views of three bioclimatic zones that coexist in nature.

A new education center featured a spreading deodar cedar that gave eager urban children a satisfying tree-climbing opportunity.

offices, gave education staff and docents more badly needed work space. Near its entrance, a large wooden deck encircled a mature deodar cedar.

The tall, spreading cedar was an immediate child magnet. They loved climbing on its lower branches, which arched gently upward. The most popular perch was an extremely robust lateral branch less than four feet above the ground.

Some staff members worried that children might reach other branches higher in the tree, then fall and hurt themselves, but Towne believed that climbing this tree could add fun and excitement to a zoo visit, especially for urban children who had limited tree-climbing opportunities. Heavy snowfall, prolonged freezing temperatures, and wind eventually cracked the branch, and it had to be removed in 2008.

The Northern Trail, designed by Jon Coe of CLR Design, Inc., and created with the support of Alaska Airlines and Brown Bear Car Wash, was opened on October 6, 1994. It featured Alaskan plants, elk, gray wolves, fishers, yellow-billed magpies, snowy owls, a brown bear, river otters, mountain goats, and bald eagles.

The exhibit offered panoramic views of three bioclimatic zones that commingle in nature—taiga, tundra,

Deadfall was placed in the bear exhibit to provide environmental enrichment and to suggest that floods helped shape the landscape.

and montane. Multiple viewpoints allowed visitors to see wolves in the foreground and elk in the background, or bears in the foreground with mountain goats in the background. Mountain goats could also be seen in the background of the river otter exhibit. The overlapping sightlines were accomplished through the use of hidden barriers placed in moats and concealed by vegetation or artificial rocks.

The wolves at the Northern Trail are often seen with elk in the background. The two species are physically separated by a hidden dry moat and a fence that is not visible to visitors.

The brown bear exhibit included a pond with viewing-through glass so visitors could get a close-up look as the bears splashed in the water. It also offered the first underwater viewing of brown bears anywhere. A glass panel inserted in a cave provided views of bears resting on a rock ledge.

A large eagle's nest was built with remnants of a bald eagle nest collected at Seattle's Discovery Park by zoo naturalist Gary Mozel. During a powerful windstorm, the nest had blown out of a tree, and portions of it were found more than 50 feet away. Mozel gathered

Designing for Bear Behavioral Enrichment

· · · · · · ·

By the time the Northern Trail exhibit was built, behavioral enrichment—giving animals stimuli similar to that in their natural environment—had become a design priority. A computerized lazy-Susan device dropped food at random times into the bear pool to attract and stimulate the animals. Live fish were provided in the bear and otter exhibits, where the animals caught and ate them in public view. Floating logs were provided in the bear pool to stimulate play and exploration. One large log was anchored with a chain at one end so the bears couldn't ram the viewing glass.

A section of the roof in the holding facility was left open so that large dead trees could be positioned to extend above the structure. Adult brown bears usually don't climb trees if they're upright but can walk on them if they are inclined. With an inclined snag extending above the roof of the holding area, bears using upper portions of the snags could reach an elevation that was high enough to allow them to smell and scan their surroundings.

As more exhibits based on the "nature as the norm" philosophy were designed and built, the overall well-being of some animals already in the zoo's collection improved. Fannie, a Kodiak bear—a subspecies of brown bear found

Brown bears continue to wade, swim, play, and even catch live fish in the Northern Trail exhibit at Woodland Park Zoo.

on Kodiak Island—had lived in the old bear grotto for many years. Fannie took her first steps in the Northern Trail in 1993, the year before the exhibit opened to the public. This was her first encounter with plants and water in a natural setting since her birth in 1970.

Staff members who had cared for her through the years and who had worked hard to bring the Northern Trail exhibit to fruition were moved to tears as she explored her new surroundings. At first, she was the only bear in the Northern Trail exhibit. But in 1995, two male cubs were added. They were brothers, born at Washington State University the year before.

Staff and volunteers were amazed that the cubs pursued, caught, and ate fish without ever having observed the fishing behavior of another bear. During their first few months in the exhibit, the bears also dug and tore up sod that had been installed in some areas. They dragged it to the pool, which soon became murky as they played with the sod in full view of the public. This was not what staff members were hoping to see, especially not the horticulture crew who had worked so hard and long to plant the exhibit. The staff replaced some of the sod and added more ground-cover plants. Eventually, the bears turned their attention to other stimuli in their environment, and most of the plantings were successfully re-established.

An off-view exercise area for bears includes a sandbox and an elevated platform. The platform provides a 360-degree vista from which bears can scan their environment.

Visitors in the Taiga Viewing Shelter can go nose-to-nose and hand-to-paw with brown bears. They are separated only by a panel of safety glass.

the nest twigs in a large bag. Eagles break twigs and small branches with their talons and arrange them with their beaks, and some of the twigs collected by Mozel showed talon and beak marks. They were stored in a garage for about a year and a half, until it was time to start building the eagle exhibit. After the eagles moved in, they rearranged some of the twigs and added a few of their own.

Eagles don't like to fly downward into dark spaces, and the designers thought it would be possible to rely on this trait to discourage the birds from flying into the open viewing area. A curtain of wire mesh was

closed when the birds were introduced to the exhibit, and it was opened by increasing increments over several days until it was fully open. The eagles preferred to use elevated perches within their part of the exhibit rather than fly downward into the viewing area. They only did so when there were no visitors.

About 1,800 zoo and aquarium professionals attended the 1995 national Association of Zoos & Aquariums conference, hosted by Woodland Park Zoo, establishing a new attendance record. The theme of the conference was nicely aligned with the values of the zoo: "Creating a sustainable future for wildlife." Nearly every volunteer and every zoo employee helped prepare for the conference, and a new zoo guide was printed in September, just in time for attendees to buy a copy. It was written by author and historian Walt Crowley and included many color photographs highlighting zoo animals and new exhibits.

The conference was a resounding success, and Woodland Park Zoo even earned AZA's best new

The zoo's exhibit team created a bald eagle nest using portions of a real nest salvaged after a windstorm at Discovery Park.

exhibit award for the Northern Trail—the first time in AZA's history that an institution hosting the conference also received the top exhibit award.

The zoo had seen big changes, and public interest and involvement was higher than ever. Zoo Society membership grew to record numbers: 32,471 households by the end of the year, an increase of 20 percent from the previous year, and attendance reached more than a million visitors a year.

Bald eagles perched high above the Northern Trail exhibit.

Saving Ivan

· · · · · · ·

The zoo had provided a home for Tusko, a mistreated elephant used for commercial purposes, back in 1932. Decades later, Ivan, a western lowland gorilla, was in need of rescue. He had lived in a Tacoma shopping mall for nearly 27 years. Ivan was one of seven gorillas captured in the Congo in 1964 to be sold to American businesses. All of the gorillas except Ivan died in transit. Before being exhibited at the mall, Ivan had spent a couple of years living at the home of a mall employee, where he was treated as a family member, like the famous Bobo.

In 1966, when Ivan became too strong and destructive to stay in a house with humans, he was moved to the mall. In the late 1980s, the Progressive Animal Welfare Society (PAWS), a group based in Lynnwood, Washington, began picketing the mall and calling for Ivan's transfer to a zoo. PAWS asserted that this would be a humane act that could also benefit science. PAWS sued Ivan's owner in March 1993, claiming that he was wrongfully using an endangered species for commercial purposes. The owner argued that the gorilla was exempt from the Endangered Species Act because he was captured before the law was passed in 1973.

RALLY FOR IVAN
SATURDAY DECEMBER 19, NOON
B&I Store · 8012 South Tacoma Way · Tacoma

Bring a sign urging Ivan's release from the B&I or use one of ours

INFO: 742-4142, ext. 611

PA🐾S

Zoo director Dave Towne negotiated with animal welfare advocates and the owner of Ivan, a gorilla who lived in a shopping mall, to find him a safe, humane home.

For more than two years, Dave Towne—known for his patience and his negotiating skills—had worked with leaders at PAWS, directors and curators at other zoos, and Ivan's owner to find a suitable, healthy environment for Ivan. There was no room for him at either Tacoma's Point Defiance or at Woodland Park Zoo in Seattle. However, Zoo Atlanta, led by Director Terry Maple, was home to 17 gorillas and had an outdoor habitat in an off-exhibit area. Here, Ivan could be gradually acclimated to the outdoors before going into an exhibit with other gorillas. With support from PAWS, Woodland Park Zoo officially received Ivan as a gift and placed him on permanent loan at Zoo Atlanta.

Local activists, gorilla experts, and many scientists from around the world as well as photographers and reporters were following the story and hoped there would be opportunities to photograph Ivan as he made his journey from Tacoma to Atlanta.

Towne felt that any stress on Ivan should be minimized. Ivan was transported in a large metal crate with ventilation holes, which did not offer much visual interest to the media. Woodland Park's senior veterinarian Dr. Janis Joslin, Zoo Atlanta's senior vice president of veterinarian services, Dr. Rita McManamon, and Ivan's keeper, Tonya Hall, accompanied him on his flight from Sea-Tac to Atlanta.

Although Ivan moved to Atlanta on October 11, 1994, it took several months to quarantine, acclimate, and socialize him with other gorillas. He walked into an outdoor naturalistic exhibit at Zoo Atlanta for the first time on March 16, 1995. Ten years later, PAWS held a special celebration to commemorate the day that Ivan took his first steps into a naturalistic exhibit.

CHAPTER SIXTEEN

DRAGONS, ORANGUTANS, AND A BABY ELEPHANT

THE TRAIL OF VINES EXHIBIT, designed by Ace Torre of Torre Design Consortium, was opened in 1996, and included lion-tailed macaques, Malayan tapirs, siamangs, and orangutans. The siamang exhibit was designed around an existing tulip tree (*Liriodendron tulipifera*), and siamangs were able to climb to a height of more than 70 feet. Their vocalizations and brachiating displays—moving from one branch to another by their swinging arms—made them especially popular.

Pathways through lush vegetation created a tropical jungle environment with plants that could live in Seattle's temperate climate. Zoo horticulture staff planted more than 6,000 individual plants representing 204 species. As with the gorilla habitats, trees were given a full growing season to take root before the powerful orangutans took up residence.

Landscaping both the Trail of Vines and Northern Trail exhibits at the same time had been a major task

LEFT: Chinta, in 2011. Woodland Park Zoo created the nation's first naturalistic exhibit for orangutans.

for the zoo's horticulture staff. By this time, the zoo had also accepted major responsibility for maintaining the Rose Garden. In 1995, All-America Rose Selections judged the zoo's rose garden as the finest of the 137 public rose gardens in the United States.

No other zoo in North America had created a naturalistic landscape for orangutans. In addition to being extremely powerful, orangutans are good climbers, and zoo professionals consider them escape artists. The zoo's orangutans had escaped twice before, and Towan once went straight to work on his cage door bolts when he found a wrench that a workman had left behind.

Now, the zoo was about to release him into an outdoor exhibit with no roof and lots of tall trees that the horticulture staff hoped would grow even taller. Trees toppled in a storm or large fallen branches can form bridges or ladders. Keepers routinely inspect the exhibits, and animals can be kept indoors while branches are removed or when new trees are added.

Orangutan keepers Helen Shewman and Libby Lawson knew that the orangutans would have to be

Later in her life, Melati was more content in the trees *inside* her exhibit.

anesthetized before they could be moved to their new exhibit. Two months before the move, they began training the animals to offer their arms to receive an injection, and the animals were immobilized without a great deal of stress. But when orangutan Towan emerged from anesthesia in his new holding facility, he pulled a door off its framework. He had to be anesthetized again and moved while the door was repaired.

No one knew if the orangutans would spend time in trees as they do in the tropical forests of Malaysia and Indonesia, using tree branches and large leaves to build sleeping nests. The orangutans took to the trees almost immediately.

Staff held their breath when orangutan Melati, who had lost a thumb in a previous accident, climbed to the top of the tallest tree in the exhibit, a deodar cedar that was estimated at nearly 75 feet. Helen Shewman, a senior keeper for orangutans at that time, wrote:

> As Melati climbed, her seven-year-old son, Heran, climbed all the way to the top of the tree after her. He was frantic when he saw her up there and tried to pull her down. This scared us half to death!
> We were all holding our breath. Fortunately, both Melati and Heran came down from the tree safely and we all breathed a collective sigh of relief.

The zoo had already gained professional recognition for caring for lion-tailed macaques. Now, it also had a new exhibit for this species where conservation messages could be presented. The Trail of Vines exhibit also provided additional space and opportunity for conservation-related information on Malayan tapirs and orangutans.

On Monday, February 12, 1996, gorilla Jumoke gave birth to a healthy 5½-pound female. The infant gorilla was named Nadiri, a Hausa word meaning "rare." This was the zoo's sixth successful gorilla birth and its first third-generation birth. Nadiri's father, Congo, had not reproduced previously, and this birth made a significant contribution to the gene pool of western lowland gorillas in zoos around the world.

Just two weeks after Nadiri was born, her father, Congo, died suddenly of a heart condition at the age of 37. Later in 1996, Congo was replaced by an adult male

Trader Towan

· · · · · · · ·

Orangutans were trained to hand over items the keepers didn't want them to have in exchange for a reward. When Towan got hold of a hose, he returned it inch by inch for a series of peanuts. When he got to the end of the hose, he snatched the whole thing back and started the negotiations anew. Zookeeper Helen Shewman hadn't realized she was only leasing the sections of hose, not buying them.

Towan also created items to trade, fashioning fake cigarettes from paper and hay, then trying to tie them together with string to offer to a keeper who smoked, first demonstrating its use by putting it in his mouth.

Towan the orangutan was a keen negotiator and businessman, even crafting items to trade for treats.

Besides being able to tie knots, orangutans are tool users. In 1996, Towan uprooted a six-foot sapling and carried it into the interior exhibit. He carefully threaded the sapling through the three-inch metal mesh above him to reach a light fixture about four feet above the top of his enclosure.

Then he used the sapling to make contact with two wing nuts that secured the light fixture. He began to loosen them—one by one—from a distance of at least six feet, even though his range of motion with the sapling was limited by the three-inch mesh. No one knows how long he worked at his task, but eventually he succeeded in loosening both wing nuts. The light fixture crashed to the mesh above his head.

Then Towan pulled out the wires and draped them around his shoulders and chest. When orangutan keeper Libby Lawson discovered what had happened, she asked Towan for the sapling and he traded it for a treat.

Towan combined trading with kindness to another species when he handed over a wild possum who had entered the area and was "playing dead." The possum was safely released.

Towan also rescued the zoo's peregrine falcon when it was temporarily stunned on a free-flight exercise in 2000. Towan picked up the bird and tried to bring it to Libby Lawson, but the falcon was trying to grab at Towan with its talons, so he put it on the ground and went to sit by Lawson at the enclosure mesh. A transfer door was opened between the two adjacent orangutan exhibits so the orangutans could be separated from the bird.

But when the door opened, Towan went back to the falcon, picked it up again, and threw it into the air. The bird was safe and unharmed. Keepers who witnessed Towan's gesture of throwing the bird in the air believe that he was attempting to help the bird become airborne again.

Concerns that the orangutans would not use the trees or vines evaporated almost immediately. Behavioral studies at the zoo showed that they were considerably more arboreal, less terrestrial, and less sedentary in their new exhibit.

named Vip (very important primate), who was to be flown from Boston to Seattle. Vip made international news when he was "bumped" from his flight due to what was described as "excessive rowdiness" in the cargo hold. The pilot and passengers of the Boeing 767 were so alarmed by the sound of Vip banging and shaking his shipping crate that he had to be removed from the plane

in Salt Lake City. Vip stayed in his crate while staff at the Hogle Zoo in Salt Lake City came to the rescue and drove him straight through to Seattle.

That same year, general curator Judy Ball and other zoo staff were trying to rescue and relocate Malayan sun bears from the overcrowded and understaffed Sepilok Forest Reserve in Malaysia. Ten Malayan sun bears were transported from Sepilok to five U.S. zoos; two of them came to Woodland Park Zoo in 1996.

Siamangs were among the species featured in the Trail of Vines exhibit, which was dedicated on June 27, 1996.

In December 1996, Woodland Park Zoo Society chairman Gerry Johnson and Zoo Society chairman-elect Phil Nudelman presented a check to the City of Seattle for $2,009,400—the last major check required to close the Zoo Society's commitment to raise $10 million in private funds to match the bond issue passed by King County voters in 1985. Bond funds helped to create five multi-acre exhibits, a new Animal Health Complex, new entry plazas, and the Seattle Rotary Education Center. In the process, the zoo earned an international reputation for its naturalistic exhibits, and no other zoo had surpassed its record of receiving AZA awards for best new exhibits.

A movement to highlight invertebrates in zoos, museums, and aquariums coincided with the rising popularity of books such as E. O. Wilson's *The Diversity of Life* (1992) and *Naturalist* (1994). Bug World opened on Halloween of 1997, and butterflies came to the zoo on May 22, 1998, in a temporary seasonal exhibit called Butterflies & Blooms that featured butterflies and moths native to North America and included an indoor walk-through area as well as outdoor plantings for Puget Sound butterfly species. In the first month more than 47,000 visitors journeyed through the exhibit.

Dave Towne had guided the zoo through a large number of impressive projects, and the 1985 zoo bond program was essentially finished in 1997. In June 1997, he was honored as the King County Municipal League's "Public Employee of the Year." Towne was also elected president of AZA—the second Woodland Park Zoo director to occupy this office. Edward Johnson had served as president of AAZPA, later AZA, in 1958.

On December 28, 1999, Woodland Park Zoo celebrated its 100th year. As part of the celebration, a time capsule was buried under the zoo's main loop path, to be opened in 2049. It is registered with an organization that supplies time capsules and documents their locations.

The late 1990s was also a time when city leaders were thinking about the next century. The mayor appointed a new Zoo Commission, known as Zoo Commission II, headed by Phil Nudelman, to make recommendations about the future of the zoo in the 21st century. The 39-member group made three significant recommendations: the zoo needed stable public funding; the future management of the zoo should be moved from the city to a nonprofit entity—something

The 1998 Butterflies & Blooms exhibit attracted more than 47,000 visitors in its first month. Shown is a spicebush swallowtail.

Species Survival Plans

· · · · · · · ·

Zoos as instruments of animal conservation had been on the minds of Woodland Park Zoo directors from the very beginning. In 1995, the Zoo Society established a Conservation Committee to provide direction and oversight to the zoo's various conservation efforts, including funding for the Center for Wildlife Conservation (CWC), led by Zoo Society president Phil Nudelman and staff scientist Sam Wasser.

CWC projects included research on stress hormones, DNA extraction, and studies of the hormonal cycles of four bear species. CWC also helped to assess the long-term impacts of poaching on African elephants in Tanzania. By the late 1990s, the zoo was also participating in 29 AZA Species Survival Plans® (SSPs).

The AZA Species Survival Plan program coordinates the efforts of AZA-accredited zoos and aquariums and related facilities and partners around the world such as the Snow Leopard Trust or the Dian Fossey Gorilla Fund International to help threatened or endangered species populations.

There are SSP programs for hundreds of species, each with its own specialized Taxon Advisory Group (TAG) of experts. SSP activities include veterinary care for wildlife diseases; establishing "assurance populations" of captive animals when they are threatened with extinction in the wild, and reintroducing them when possible; managing studbooks and breeding and transfer plans to promote healthy genetic diversity in zoo populations; and establishing contraceptive programs for animals who shouldn't be bred. SSP manuals compile animal care and management knowledge from biologists, veterinarians, nutritionists, reproduction physiologists, behaviorists, researchers, and TAGs. Woodland Park Zoo coordinated the sun bear, sloth bear, and lion-tailed macaque SSPs.

many zoos had done successfully; and the zoo should invest more in education and wildlife conservation.

In 2000, after a long and eventful career as a City employee, Dave Towne retired as director of the zoo. Former deputy director Mike Waller became acting director. Towne would continue working with Waller to shape the future of the zoo, remaining at the helm of the Zoo Society as executive director and CEO until 2002.

As noted by the new commission led by Phil Nudelman, many other zoos around the country had already moved to nonprofit management, and Woodland Park Zoo was headed that way. Under Towne's leadership, the Zoo Society, led by Maggie Walker and Dale Sperling, would organize itself to manage the zoo's entire operation. Acting director Mike Waller continued to work closely with Dave Towne to address the internal demands of their two organizations and develop a transition plan for the management of the zoo. City Parks Superintendent Ken Bounds and budget director Dwight Dively were instrumental in guiding this complex transition.

Significant new births in 2000 included a Malayan tapir, three snow leopards, two red-crowned cranes, the zoo's first kea hatching (a species of parrot), a wild goat called a serow, and a female gorilla. But the most exciting birth was a female Asian elephant born on November 3. Her mother, Chai, had been sent to Dickerson Park Zoo in Springfield, Missouri, to breed with a bull elephant named Onyx.

This was the first elephant born at Woodland Park Zoo and the first to be born anywhere in the state of Washington. The population of elephants in zoos had been on a steady decline, and this birth contributed to the gene pool.

A "name the baby elephant" contest followed, with more than 15,000 submissions. Mayor Schell announced

Tree Kangaroo Conservation Program

· · · · · · ·

In 1996, Dr. Lisa Dabek and zookeeper Judy Steenberg launched the zoo's Tree Kangaroo Conservation Program (TKCP), focused on the endangered Matschie's tree kangaroo (*Dendrolagus matschiei*) and the rain forest habitat in which it lives, on the Huon Peninsula in Papua New Guinea. TKCP began by assessing how the tree kangaroos were doing in the wild. Over the decades it evolved into a holistic program supporting habitat protection for a wide range of threatened species, as well as initiatives to enhance local community livelihoods and access to government services.

In 2009, TKCP worked with local landowners to help create Papua New Guinea's first ever Conservation Area, officially recognized by the national government. Landowners pledged more than 180,000 acres of rain forest habitat for the protection of tree kangaroos and other species of the Huon Peninsula. By uniting landowners, government officials, and conservation partners, TKCP had created a community of advocates to address long-term management for the Conservation Area. They work with local communities to save the animals and the forest resources they share and increase economic opportunities for the surrounding communities in order to reduce pressure on the habitat.

Lisa Dabek, who has authored and presented many scholarly papers on tree kangaroos, went on to become Woodland Park Zoo's first conservation director in 2004. She has since worked with more than 30 conservation projects to save endangered species—from snow leopards to elephants. The *Seattle P-I* wrote of Dabek, "Deep in her heart, she's a serious marsupial groupie—a researcher of such patience and passion she's called the 'Jane Goodall of tree kangaroos.' "

the winning name—Hansa—on live TV. Hansa means "supreme happiness" in the Thai language. The contest winner, 6½-year-old Madison Gordon, appeared on NBC's *Today* show with Matt Lauer.

Zoo attendance skyrocketed. Hansa's first steps, her first swim, and her first birthday cake—made of corn-meal mush and mashed potatoes—all made the news. During Hansa's first year of life, a record 1.2 million people visited the zoo, and a special circulation route was devised to manage the crowds.

The Dragons of Komodo exhibit proved surprisingly popular. It opened on May 27, 2000, in the old Feline House, now named the Adaptations Building.

Acting director Mike Waller with Hansa, 2001.

Hansa was the first elephant to be born at Woodland Park Zoo and the first anywhere in the state of Washington. She weighed 235 pounds at birth in November 2000.

The arrival of the super-sized Komodo lizards was advertised on the sides of buses with the caption "shown actual size." Twenty thousand visitors saw the exhibit during the first two days, waiting in line for up to two hours. Reptile curator Dana Payne wrote, "The lizards did their part, moving about and remaining visible . . . not the usual reptile lifestyle mode at all."

In 2000, the zoo's senior veterinarian Darin Collins, general curator Judy Ball, and keeper Cheryl Frederick traveled to Indonesia to acquire one of 10 Malayan sun bears that were wild caught and had been in private hands illegally. One bear came to Woodland Park Zoo, while the others went to other AZA-accredited institutions in North America.

That same year, the zoo completed its first year of work on the Ferruginous Hawk Field Study, a cooperative project with the Washington Department of Fish and Wildlife. Among other things, it was discovered that ferruginous hawk populations migrate across the Continental Divide instead of being two discrete populations. This important finding helped to create more accurate management plans for the birds and their prey.

With a new exhibit and a baby elephant, the zoo was definitely on the public's mind when voters were asked to support the zoo by voting for the $198.2 million Seattle Pro Parks Levy in November 2000. The eight-year levy passed and brought the zoo $21 million in operating support, technology upgrades, education support, subsidies for low-income student admissions, and maintenance funds. This funding supported the most recent Zoo Commission goal of stable zoo funding.

There was help from elsewhere, too. During a visit to the zoo, Microsoft billionaire Bill Gates and his family couldn't find the entrance to the African Savanna. They weren't the only ones. Other visitors had also missed the right path. The zoo wanted to create a "sense of entry" to the African Savanna, and an African Gateway Village, funded by the Bill and Melinda Gates Foundation, opened on Memorial Day weekend of 2001.

Planners suggested building a small rural village at the edge of a wildlife sanctuary or similar undeveloped landscape. The zoo staff consulted many experts, including several who were living in East Africa. Focus group sessions were conducted with African American staff members, educators, and other members of Seattle's African American community.

The zoo hired architect Pat Janikowski, who designed several authentic Kikuyu structures within which the zoo staff could offer interpretive programs and display objects from daily life in rural East Africa.

The zoo was pleased that the project offered an opportunity to apply "cultural resonance" to an existing exhibit zone, connecting the natural habitat with the culture of the people living nearby, as well as helping visitors find their way around.

African Gateway Village was completed in 2001 and provided a more prominent entry to the African Savanna.

CHAPTER SEVENTEEN

A Fox Sails South, Gordo Takes a Dip, Ponies Ride Off into the Sunset

ON APRIL 29, 2002, Dr. Deborah Jensen took over as president and CEO of the Woodland Park Zoological Society. Both Mike Waller and Dave Towne stayed on to assist in the transition, working with board co-chairs Maggie Walker and Bill Lewis. The zoo had launched a nationwide search for someone who would be the first executive to run the zoo under nonprofit management and who would help develop the education and conservation work of the zoo while ensuring financial security. They wanted someone who was eager to work with people and organizations doing fieldwork on the habitats and species represented at the zoo, and Jensen was both a conservation and biodiversity expert. She had a doctoral degree, had authored or co-authored many scientific publications, and had worked at the Nature Conservancy as vice president of the environmental group's Conservation Science Division.

LEFT: The range of species at the zoo continued to grow over the years, including insects such as this flamboyant flower beetle.

When Jensen heard of the opening, she spoke with contacts at the Bronx Zoo, and at the Brookfield Zoo and Lincoln Park Zoo in Chicago. She reported later that they all told her the Woodland Park Zoo was one of the best in the nation "and likely one of the best in the world" and that "if she was interested she'd better treat the application process seriously."

Deborah Jensen.

Jensen had been at the zoo for less than three months when she dedicated the new African Wild Dog exhibit on June 28, 2002. The exhibit represented a stream-bed bordered by high mud banks. Visitors could see the animals from different vantage points, including a cave

The African Wild Dog exhibit was added to the zoo's African Savanna exhibit in 2002.

view to a heated underground den. Woodland Park Zoo's first African wild dogs were four male littermates born at Chicago's Brookfield Zoo. Dr. John W. "Tico" McNutt, a Seattle native and wild dog expert who had studied five generations of wild dogs in Botswana, helped prepare the exhibit, and the zoo committed to provide financial support for his project.

In 2002, the zoo hosted a Snow Leopard Survival Summit, with people from 11 of the 12 countries where snow leopards lived. The summit discussed protecting snow leopards from extinction by giving people who lived near them ways to earn a living that did not involve hunting or other activities that threatened the species. The following year, ZooStore manager Terry Blumer traveled to Central Asia with representatives of the International Snow Leopard Trust (ISLT) to help develop and market moneymaking handicrafts known as "conservation goods."

When Jensen arrived in Seattle, the zoo was in the midst of changing the way it managed elephants from "free contact" to "protected contact." Historically, the zoo had allowed for hands-on contact, keepers riding an elephant in the Thai logging demonstration, and children's rides on elephants.

By 2002, many North American zoos were making this change, which required some form of barrier between elephants and keepers at all times. Several injuries caused by elephants occurred during the zoo's history; some required medical attention, but none were fatal. Protected contact makes working around elephants safer, and it also means that managing elephant behavior occurs almost entirely through positive motivation and rewards.

The elephant crew was also preparing to transport Asian elephant Sri to the Saint Louis Zoo on a permanent breeding loan. And they were doing what they could to improve two-year-old Hansa's relationship with the other elephants. Bamboo, one of the zoo's Asian elephants, had shown aggression toward her.

In January 2003, the media was on hand as Hansa was being weighed. She was approaching an elephant milestone—her first ton. In less than three years, Hansa had gained more than 1,750 pounds. She was also extremely active most of the time, often playing with a behavioral-enrichment object known as a boomer ball—a large thick-walled plastic ball made for zoo animals.

Hansa loved to play with toys.

Other animals had boomer balls too, but because of the zoo's emphasis on naturalistic exhibits, they were typically kept in areas off view to the public. People could watch Hansa play with her ball because much of the Elephant Forest exhibit included architecture that suggested that many elephants in Thailand live among people, and it also included objects from the world of humans.

Two female Sumatran tiger cubs made their public debut in 2003, and were the first to be born at the zoo since 1992.

On December 16, 2002, two female Sumatran tigers were born. To ensure that the cubs and mother bonded properly and all were healthy, the tigers were kept in a quiet, well-heated environment. This meant that they would be off view until the following spring.

In early 2003, a video monitor was installed in the Adaptations Building (formerly the Feline House) so that visitors could see the tiger cubs. The cubs made their public debut in an indoor exhibit on Saturday, March 29, and were introduced to their outdoor exhibit when the weather was warm enough. Ballots with a list of Indonesian names allowed more than 10,000 people to decide what to call the cubs. On April 25, the zoo announced the winning names: Jaya (jie-yah), meaning "freedom," and Suriya (soo-ree-ya), meaning "sun."

The Northern Trail exhibit apparently appeared completely natural to a pair of wild eagles who showed up in 2002 and built a nest in the elk area. They successfully raised two young at this nest site in 2002 and 2003.

When Jaguar Cove opened on June 28, 2003, it was the first exhibit to include underwater views of a swimming jaguar. Gordo, the zoo's jaguar, had spent most of his life in comparatively small enclosures in the Adaptations Building. He was born at the

Gordo's new exhibit was approximately four times larger than his previous enclosure.

Woodland Park Zoo was the first in North America to open an exhibit that offered underwater viewing of a swimming jaguar. The pool depth can be regulated up to four feet at the viewing glass. Fish provide behavioral stimulation and a dietary supplement in both the pool and stream.

zoo in 1994 and named after longtime feline keeper Gordon Swanberg.

Gordo appeared to enjoy the pools in that building, but had never been in water deep enough to allow swimming. In the wild, jaguars are rarely found very far from water and are good swimmers. Gordo put his feet in the shallow stream but generally preferred to cross it on an artificial log. Although he occasionally splashed and waded, he did not seem very interested in going for a swim or catching live fish.

Two years later, the zoo was submitting Jaguar Cove for an AZA exhibit award. Without photos of a swimming jaguar, the application wouldn't be competitive. By offering some favorite treats at the right time, staff members lured Gordo into the water and some images were obtained just in time to meet AZA's deadline. After that, Gordo and other jaguars went swimming more often, thanks to a bequest from board member Rick Buckley for the jaguar exhibit and for conservation in the wild.

As 2003 came to a close, the 1911 Primate House was finally demolished. It was being used for storage and keeper office space. There was a move to save the old building, but the Landmarks Preservation Board voted on February 19, 2003, to deny the nomination of the Primate House for landmark preservation.

In 2004, zoo entomologist Erin Sullivan reported that Bug World received more phone calls and questions about spiders than anything else. Zoo leadership decided to create a spider exhibit, and Sullivan helped design it. She wrote:

> *It has been a little difficult to get staff interested in this new exhibit because it focuses on something I think people have an innate fear of. However, I am sure that when staff first see the spiders, they'll appreciate their beauty and importance.*

The Bug World building was slightly remodeled and filled with spider information. Across the plaza, another exhibit presented a mock courtroom in which Sammy the Spider Stomper, accused of stomping on spiders without considering how much they contributed to the well-being of humans and ecosystems, was placed on trial in The Zooperior Court of

Arctic Stowaway

· · · · · · ·

When Cooter Whitaker, a terminal manager for Samson Tug and Barge at the Port of Seattle, opened a container in the company's shipyard in Seattle one day, he discovered a fox sitting on a mound of debris. The male arctic fox had found his way into a ship's trash container during a port stop on the Aleutian island of Shemya, and arrived at the zoo on May 29, 2004, after spending five days at sea.

He weighed in at 5.8 pounds, half the weight of an average adult arctic fox, and he was glassy eyed, loaded with parasites, weak in the hindquarters, and had bad teeth. He appeared to be middle-aged, somewhere between three and five years old.

He wasn't a good candidate for release. Non-native to the state of Washington, he was not legally allowed to be released anywhere nearby. Arctic foxes are abundant in Alaska, and a trip back to Alaska might be stressful and would certainly be expensive.

Somer arrived to join Feliks at the zoo in 2005.

Arctic fox in the Northern Trail exhibit.

The zoo happened to have an empty enclosure at the Northern Trail exhibit. After a rather long quarantine period, he gained his weight and strength back. The arctic fox was released into the care of the Northern Trail keepers. He settled into exhibit life immediately. He became surprisingly playful and was described in the Keeper's Daily Reports as a "joy to work with" and "an amazing little guy." Soon he would go into "play bows" when his keepers approached, and toss toys in the air and then pounce on them when they landed. He was named Feliks, which means "happy" in Russian.

In the spring of 2005 he got unusually active. Restlessly moving throughout his exhibit, he even started climbing up the mesh sides of his enclosure and testing the perimeter. Within a few days he started yipping and vocalizing during his morning endeavors. It soon became clear that spring was in the air and Feliks was trying to find a mate. The staff confirmed that these behaviors were consistent with arctic fox biology in the wild. Sara Manetti, Northern Trail keeper, said, "Soon we found ourselves in the curator's office pleading Feliks' case." Feliks' companion, Somer, came from the Maryland Zoo and arrived in Seattle on October 27, 2005.

When spiders were added to the collection, some zookeepers found it easier than others to overcome their arachnophobia.

Spider Justice. While the exhibit changed some minds, a few staff members were never really able to conquer their arachnophobia.

In 2004, the zoo board and executive staff, after much deliberation, created a mission statement that made clear how it viewed its role under new, unified management. "Woodland Park Zoo saves animals and their habitats through conservation leadership and engaging experiences, inspiring people to learn, care, and act."

The zoo was involved with 38 conservation projects in more than 27 countries, and in 2004, Dr. Lisa Dabek became the first conservation director. She was already well known at the zoo. Under her direction, the Tree Kangaroo Conservation Program had been working in Papua New Guinea since 1996.

The zoo was also offering programs on practical conservation for city dwellers, including Natural Lawn and Garden Care, Worm Bins, Bat Houses, and Bird Houses. Education programs reached nearly 100,000 students in 2004, both in programming at the zoo and outreach into the community.

On October 11, 2004, the City Council passed the zoo's Long-Range Physical Development Plan, covering the next 20 years. It was prepared by Jon Coe and Gary Lee of CLR Design. The zoo's overall layout and its naturalistic approach remained essentially unchanged from the original 1976 master plan prepared by Jones & Jones. In fact, major portions of that plan were excerpted without any changes in the zoo's new documents, a tribute to the vision and direction that remained valid 30 years later.

The new plan paid significant attention to the visitor experience. Dave Towne had hired visitor experience researchers, and the zoo knew that visitors wanted more contact with zoo staff members who could answer questions, more interaction with the animals, and improvements to visitor amenities such as places to sit and rest. Visitors also complained that animals were hard to see, a common problem at zoos that give animals a wide range of location choices within an enclosure.

The zoo had been working on plans for a new mixed-species exhibit that would guarantee high animal visibility and bring visitors very close to certain animals. Willawong Station was an indoor enclosure that had been occupied by tree kangaroos and much earlier by giraffes. Now, visitors could enter the exhibit where parakeets and other birds were flying freely, and they could also pay a dollar for a feed stick, so they could feed the birds without touching them. Willawong is an Aboriginal word meaning "the junction of two streams," places that are often filled with trees and birds. The name was also chosen to reinforce the association with Australasia, the thematic zone in which the exhibit was located.

In January 2006, Jensen announced the end of pony rides. At this time the zoo had only a small, aging herd, hardly up to the job of lugging kids around in a circle. If the zoo refreshed the pony herd with new animals, the old animals would first need to be placed

The Willawong Station exhibit let visitors and Australasian birds mingle.

in new homes because of the physical limitations of the pony barn and paddock. Jensen could not justify the time, effort, and expense of starting over with a new herd and then placing the animals somewhere off-site at the end of the season. The zoo's plan called for a new pony ring to be physically associated with the Family Farm, but this would require raising $3 million.

The pony ring had been in operation since 1914, and many generations of children had ridden the zoo's ponies and volunteered as pony leaders. Some zoo staff members had begun their careers as paid pony attendants. Now, Jensen had something else in mind for children, even toddlers. On May 19, 2006, the long-planned indoor educational playground, Zoomazium, where 21st-century children would lay down their own generation's memories of the zoo, opened to an enthusiastic reception.

CHAPTER EIGHTEEN

A New Place for Kids, an Old-Fashioned Carousel, and an Untimely Death

ZOOMAZIUM, DESIGNED BY DAVID GOLDBERG of the Mithun architectural firm, took some of the sting out of the end of the pony ring. It was designed to address the "nature deficit" in the lives of 21st-century children who weren't climbing trees, playing in woods and vacant lots, or observing animals and plants in their habitats as much as previous generations of children had.

Other facilities at the zoo had been designed with the assumption that the adults in a family group would interpret and generally guide the learning experiences of children. Zoomazium was aimed squarely at children themselves, giving them what they needed to learn through their own play. Children loved it.

The zoo's long-range plan included the idea of a "winter zoo," a place where families could come when the weather wasn't so great. Zoomazium was a key part of that plan. And it worked. When yearly attendance was about 1.2 million, 450,000 people came through Zoomazium, mainly in the winter months. It provided

ABOVE: On May 5, 2005, Deborah Jensen and Mayor Greg Nickels joined schoolchildren to break ground for Zoomazium.

year-round, whole-body activities that would help children connect with nature, even when it was cold and rainy outdoors, and Zoomazium's Nature Exchange program allowed thousands of children to bring in something they had found in nature and ask naturalists all about it.

LEFT: It's hard to top the appeal of mothers and babies to zoo visitors.

Zoomazium opened on May 19, 2006, and occupies almost exactly the same footprint as the 1911 Primate House (Simianary), which was removed in late 2003.

Earth-friendly innovations at Zoomazium, the first Leadership in Energy and Environmental Design (LEED) Gold zoo building in the United States, included a roof covered with growing native plants to reduce stormwater runoff and the use of recycled and forest-friendly materials. Zoomazium was also one of the first buildings in the nation to use fritting, a new technology to prevent birds from flying into windows and killing or injuring themselves. Fritting uses a pattern of white dots on windows that can be seen from outside by birds in flight, but not from inside by people.

In 2005, the zoo added a new event at the Northern Trail—Bear Affair—which became an annual event.

It taught visitors about bears in the wild and how to camp safely in bear country. Camping equipment, including pots and pans, a hammock, a cooler, and a bear bag to store food away from scavenging bears, was all provided by outdoor gear retailer Recreational Equipment, Inc. For the bears it was another enrichment activity. For attendees it was a memorable lesson in proper food storage while camping in a wildlife habitat. The zoo was also developing a reputation for its wildlife preservation work. In July 2006, the *Seattle Times'* Lynne Varner wrote a story about the zoo's role as "ambassador for the wild," describing the zoo's commitment to species conservation and preservation of wildlife habitat.

On Saturday, July 22, 2006, the zoo's Historic Carousel went into operation inside a new pavilion dedicated to former zoo director and parks superintendent Dave Towne. It had been officially accepted by Towne in December 2000 from donors Tom and Linda Allen, who wanted to bring a complete historic carousel to Seattle. The Allens arranged for the carousel to be restored to its original condition, and fundraising began for the $800,000 pavilion in which to house it.

In 2005, the zoo added Bear Affair to its offering of annual events and programs. This photo was taken in the zoo's Northern Trail exhibit during an event training campers on bear safety.

Carousels Go Round and Round and Come and Go

An exception to the modern no-rides policy, the historic carousel was part of a long tradition.

There had been complaints when rides were removed from the zoo in 1980. The zoo was being purged of anything that resembled carnivals or encouraged the idea that the role of zoos was primarily to show children a good time, rather than educate the public. Critics felt that the good old days were over. But when Dave Towne agreed to accept the historic carousel in 2000, there were complaints that adding this feature would take the zoo back to what some regarded as the bad old days of zoo rides.

Dana Payne, editor of the zoo's internal newsletter, wrote:

Let's say you're the zoo director and you're generally opposed to having amusement park rides at the zoo, but . . . You find one that's free (donated), a thing of beauty, a historical treasure of sorts and therefore possessed of a certain dignity, doesn't take up a lot of space (you can stick it in a building), not excessively noisy, not the sort of ride that induces adrenaline rushes, can operate year-round (unlike pony rides or the contact area), would be loved by children and adults alike (adding to the zoo's fun factor), and finally it's projected to net a quarter million dollars a year (which will be earmarked specifically for education and animal care, in addition to current allocations). Hmmm. What would you do? (Dana Payne, ZOOBULLETIN, Vol. 12 #12, Nov. 27, 2000)

Carousels had a long history at the zoo. In 1919, George E. Vincent and his wife, Lucy, began operating an amusement park with a carousel at 5501 Phinney Avenue, just across the street from the zoo. On the evening of August 26, 1934, the carousel, Ferris wheel, skating rink, and concession stand were all destroyed in a spectacular fire that drew crowds of curious spectators.

Sometime after March 1940, Fern Huggins installed a carousel at the zoo and agreed to pay 15 percent of her profits to the City. After several weeks of low yields, the Board of Parks Commissioners asked for a 5 percent increase in the percentage of profits that would go to the City. Huggins decided to take her carousel and leave, and by July it was gone.

In 1950 the Board of Parks Commissioners allowed John Beck to install children's rides in an area of the zoo that was to be known as Kiddyland. One of the rides was a "jumping merry-go-round." Different concessionaires with different rides held the zoo's Kiddyland concession over the next 20 years. The rides often included a carousel or merry-go-round of some kind.

Carnival Sales Company, owned by Benjamin Meyers, held the Kiddyland concession from 1958 until the early 1970s. An article in the *Seattle Times* on June 18, 1961, said that the carousel then operating at Woodland Park Zoo, with 76 wooden horses and its original band organ, was of German manufacture and had recently been moved to the zoo from Coney Island. By 1980, the last Kiddyland concession contract expired and the rides were gone.

Kiddyland rides were a big part of a baby boomer zoo visit, but were phased out by 1980.

The historic carousel, honoring director Dave Towne, became a revenue generator and a child magnet.

Although a lot of people thought it was returning to the zoo after a long absence, the carousel had never been at Woodland Park Zoo. It was first installed at the Cincinnati Zoo in 1918 and later sold to a park in Santa Clara, California, where it operated until 1996. The carousel is catalogued among historic carousels as PTC #45, which means that it was the 45th carousel built by the Philadelphia Toboggan Company (PTC). The Philadelphia Toboggan Company was known for its high standards of engineering and the quality of its carved horses, most of them hand-carved by John Zalar.

The carved wooden horses weren't the only new arrivals. A Sumatran tiger cub born at the zoo on December 12, 2006, was cause for celebration, as this subspecies is very rare in the wild. New additions to

the African Savanna included birds, goats, guinea fowl, and arthropods. Ostriches made their first appearance at the zoo in more than 40 years, and artificial ostrich eggs and simulated termite mounds were added as educational props.

On May 1, 2007, visitors began to feed giraffes from a platform along a new section of pathway at the Savanna. Visitors paid $5 for this up-close, staff-supervised experience, and both children and adults were delighted as the giraffes' heads loomed calmly toward the branches in their outstretched hands. The experience gave visitors a close-up look that helped them appreciate the scale of one of the planet's megafauna species. Other up-close feeding experiences were developed for penguins in 2009 and elephants in 2011.

In 2007, Kakuta Hamisi was hired as coordinator of the Cultural Interpreter Program, at the African Village entry to the Savanna. Hamisi had worked seasonally at the zoo for six years because of his firsthand knowledge of cultural and ecological aspects of savanna habitat in East Africa. Three more men from Kenya were hired as cultural interpreters for the summer of 2007. They shared firsthand stories of life on the savanna, their relationship with wildlife, efforts to retain their cultural heritage, and conservation issues. Hamisi had helped curate the exhibit back in 2001, and had worked as an interpreter there every summer since then. The interpretive programs were promoted collectively as Maasai Journey.

That summer, the zoo was taken aback when critics complained that the program reinforced a racist perception of Africans as subhuman. Eric Ames, an assistant professor of Germanics who had studied a German zoo with a similar exhibit, talked about the history of zoos bringing in people of color as accessories to exhibits, and said the Maasai Journey was "a contemporary example of the exoticism of Africa," part of a ghastly history of exhibiting African people along with animals. In 1906, the Bronx Zoo had exhibited a Congolese man named Ota Benga in a cage with an orangutan.

Feeding the giraffes provides visitors with the human–animal contact that is central to the popularity of zoos.

Hamisi and his colleagues disagreed. He and other staff members attended a public forum organized by University of Washington students and professors at the Langston Hughes Performing Arts Center. The zoo's position was that saving animals and their habitats and saving human cultures went hand in hand, and that cultural interpretation was part of its role as an advocate for conservation. The term "cultural resonance" had been coined to describe Woodland Park Zoo's approach to exhibit design back in the 1980s when it created the Thai Village within the Elephant Forest exhibit.

Hamisi and his colleagues saw their work as enhancing social and cultural understanding, and as part of the partnership with the zoo that promoted conservation in Kenya and related work with local communities there.

After the forum, representatives of the zoo and its critics discussed their positions on the local NPR radio affiliate, KUOW, but they never reached consensus. Stephanie Camp, associate professor of history at the University of Washington, was a zoo member who loved taking her toddler son to the zoo. She said she was "surprised and shocked to see representation of African human life and people at the zoo," and said children were asking why there were African people at the zoo, "a place they go to see animals."

But the zoo thought of itself as much more than a place to see animals. In response, conservation director Dr. Lisa Dabek said that the zoo's job was not just to show animals to people, but also to show the people in relation to the animals nearby, and to promote conservation in partnership with them. Dabek had pioneered this approach in her years of work as a field biologist with the zoo's partnership to learn about and save tree kangaroos in Papua New Guinea, which led to a close working relationship with the people who shared the kangaroos' forest home.

Interpreters Kobole and Sokoine engage visitors at the hippo exhibit.

Camp's response was that while the zoo's intentions to "show the natural world holistically" might be "admirable," the zoo should represent either a variety of cultures and people and races or none. Of course, for many years, the zoo had shown photos and illustrations on exhibit signs of indigenous people from Thailand, Indonesia, and Alaska. Representatives of indigenous cultures participated in certain zoo events and educational programs but had not worked as zoo staff members in connection with specific exhibit zones. Cultural resonance had come with controversy and confusion as the zoo's attempts at cultural inclusion had somehow backfired.

In the spring of 2007, Woodland Park Zoo was certified as a Backyard Wildlife Habitat by both the Washington Department of Fish and Wildlife and the National Wildlife Federation. Teachers, volunteers, and zoo staff celebrated by taking part in a Backyard Habitat workshop on Earth Day to plant trees and shrubs at the zoo. In 2007, the zoo's botanical collection consisted of more than 92,000 plants representing more than 1,000 species. Thanks to its embrace of native horticulture, more than 165 wild species of birds had been seen at Woodland Park Zoo by 2010.

Early in the morning of June 8, 2007, juvenile elephant Hansa, 6½ years old, died, lying in the stall next to her mother, Chai. Hansa and Chai usually slept together. The other elephants, Watoto and Bamboo, were allowed to visit her body for a while because elephants in the wild are known to stand vigil for hours or even days when a member of the herd dies.

Several days earlier Hansa had shown a slight decrease in appetite and activity, and the staff conducted numerous tests, monitored her closely, and gave her fluids and antibiotics. She had improved and appeared to be stabilizing. The elephant barn was closed for the rest of the day, zoo-goers were told at the main gates what had happened, and a necropsy was performed in the afternoon.

Hansa died of a previously unknown elephant herpesvirus. It was a form of Asian and African elephant endotheliotropic herpesviruses (EEHV), but was genetically different and couldn't be detected in established tests. Every elephant in the wild or in human care carries one or more forms of elephant herpesvirus.

Hundreds of condolence notes and cards arrived at the zoo from all over the world. Staff and volunteers held a private gathering to share them. A professional grief counselor was hired to work with staff and volunteers.

The zoo remained committed to trying to breed another elephant. Only 30,000 to 50,000 Asian elephants remained in the wild, scattered across fragmented habitats in 13 countries. Chai was artificially inseminated 10 times from 2005 to 2012 using the noninvasive ultrasound-guided protocol developed by the Institute for Zoo and Wildlife Research in Berlin in collaboration with the Smithsonian's National Zoo. While Chai was pregnant in 2008, she unfortunately experienced a miscarriage early in the pregnancy.

In 2010, general curator Dr. Nancy Hawkes, a reproductive physiologist and co-principal on the assisted reproduction research at Smithsonian, said, "Chai is healthy and in excellent condition for pregnancy. Elephants are very social animals that live in multigenerational herds. Another baby for Chai would be socially enriching for her and the herd and would help us begin to rebuild a multigenerational social group here at Woodland Park Zoo."

Animal-rights activists were speculating about the causes of Hansa's death. Some of them argued that elephants should never be kept in zoos. Others wanted to abolish zoos altogether. It was a controversy that had been brewing for some time. While elephants had been a beloved symbol of all that was most joyous about zoos, there had long been some opposition to exhibiting them. The zoo had received its first known complaint about exhibiting elephants in 1962, and there had been a subsequent controversy about accepting Hansa's mother, Chai, as a gift. The controversy was not over.

Hansa playing with a barrel. Her death sparked an outpouring of grief, and questions from animal-rights activists.

CHAPTER NINETEEN

FLAMINGOS, PENGUINS, AND LIGHTS OUT FOR THE NIGHT EXHIBIT

BY 2007, it looked as if the struggle to provide more parking at the zoo—a struggle that had gone on since the era of the Model T Ford—was finally near its end. The design was approved, the funds were there, and a permit to go ahead and start building was granted on June 18. But on July 2, opponents filed an appeal against the City's decision to issue the permit, and by October 29 the project was halted. A survey indicated that only 34 percent of the people living nearby were in favor of the garage. Jensen decided that maintaining good relations with the neighbors was important, and the zoo began experimenting with bus shuttles.

In January 2008, a specialized medical team of neurosurgeons and a neonatologist from Seattle's Children's Hospital joined the zoo's Animal Health staff to remove a growth overlying the spine of a female gorilla born the preceding fall. This congenital condition, a form of spina bifida, while found in human infants, had never

been reported in gorillas. The infant recovered well from the surgery, and a few months later she was named Uzumma, which means "bearer of joy to the family."

Two ocelot cubs were born in September, the first time in 15 years that this endangered cat species had reproduced at the zoo. They were the offspring of a new male ocelot received in the spring of 2008. A number of other new animals were added to the zoo's collection in 2008, including a female snow leopard, a male lowland gorilla, and a male De Brazza's guenon—a species of monkey.

On May 24, 2008, a new flamingo exhibit opened. Nick and DeEtte Johnson had given the zoo 27 Chilean flamingos in 2006. The birds had been living in a holding pen at the zoo for about a year and a half while an exhibit was designed and built by zoo staff. It included a shallow pool bordered by a simulated mud bank typical of saline estuaries along the Chilean coast, and replicas of flamingo nests, complete with feathers stuck to them. An artificial egg sat on top of two of the nests, while the third nest had no egg. Instead, there

LEFT: The strong human desire to establish eye contact with another species is a big part of the zoo experience.

were tiny flamingo footprints leading away from it. A marketing campaign included outdoor billboards, scooter riders in flamingo-themed attire, and flocks of plastic flamingos.

The following spring, the flamingos put on a striking synchronized courtship show—head flagging, wing saluting, and marching in sequence and unison, followed by nest building. The flamingo eggs were artificially incubated and the chicks were hand-reared, primarily to reduce the risk of predation by local raccoons and crows.

There were multiple hatchings of Chilean flamingo chicks in 2009. It was the first time this species had reproduced at the zoo.

There were many more new arrivals. On May 25, 2009, twin snow leopards were born—one male and one female. They made their public debut on August 14. On February 13, 2009, four laughing kookaburras and two tawny frogmouths arrived from the Taronga Zoo in Sydney, Australia. Kookaburras hatched in June and October, and a tawny frogmouth chick hatched on June 4.

A tawny frogmouth chick hatched at Woodland Park Zoo on June 4, 2009. It was the first hatching of this species at the zoo. Only four zoos in North America had successfully bred this species during the preceding six years.

On May 9, 2009, a male red-crowned crane hatched at the zoo—the most recent of more than a dozen offspring from a pair of cranes that began reproducing at the zoo in 1999. Other new animals in 2009 included a female giraffe, a pair of northern tree shrews (a new species for Woodland Park Zoo), and a male Matschie's tree kangaroo. Matschie's tree kangaroos had been absent from the zoo's collection since 2006 but were still the subject of one of the zoo's most ambitious conservation partnerships in Papua New Guinea. *National Geographic* and *ABC News* joined conservation director Lisa Dabek and her team for the first filming of endangered tree kangaroos collared zoo's environmental practices as part of a master's project. They wrote a "zoo footprint" report that detailed the zoo's water-use, carbon, waste, and energy. After this study, the zoo set some ambitious environmental goals. So when zoo COO Bruce Bohmke started working with Hanson|Roberts, he asked them to consider filling the penguin pool "once, and never again," asking, "Can we do that?" The result was a design that reduced penguin exhibit water use by 3 million gallons a year by using a series of filtration devices and a wetland outside the exhibit for the final filtration.

Although most people associate all penguin species with ice and snow, Humboldts live along the desert coastline and islands of Peru and Chile. In 2009, only

Another red-crowned crane chick hatched at Woodland Park Zoo in 2009. The red-crowned crane is the second-most-endangered crane species.

with Crittercams, a research tool that helps scientists study a species' habitat needs.

The new Humboldt penguin exhibit, designed by the Hanson|Roberts design firm, opened to the public with special festivities on Saturday, May 2, 2009, including South American music, keeper talks, Peruvian storytelling, and penguin-themed giveaways. The exhibit was funded by an anonymous donor who had given the zoo its largest donation ever—six million dollars—in addition to other private and public support.

Two years earlier, a student study group from the University of Washington had done a review of the

The zoo's conservation partnerships in Papua New Guinea focused on habitat needs of Matschie's tree kangaroos.

The 2009 penguin exhibit replicated the desert coast of Peru's Punta San Juan.

an estimated 12,000 Humboldt penguins still survived in the wild. One of the greatest threats to their survival is overfishing of anchovies, the penguin's primary food source. At this time most of the anchovies in Humboldt feeding habitat were caught for the pet-food market. Other human activities such as harvesting guano deposits, in which Humboldt penguins build nests, also posed a threat. In 2009, the zoo began to contribute financially to the Humboldt Penguin Conservation Center in Punta San Juan, Peru.

Three weeks before the exhibit opened, 20 penguins of various ages arrived from several different zoos and aquariums. The birds went through the zoo's standard quarantine for newly arrived animals in the exhibit's interior enclosure. When they were introduced to the new exhibit, they immediately took to the water. As of

2016, more than 55 Humboldt penguins had been born in this exhibit, overseen by bird curator Mark Myers.

The 17,000-square-foot exhibit replicated the desert coast of Punta San Juan—home of Peru's largest Humboldt penguin colony. With simulated cliffs, rocky tide pools, crashing waves, and a beach, this shoreline exhibit provided a dramatic contrast to the terrestrial animal exhibits found throughout much of the zoo. The zoo was awarded the 2010 Exhibit Achievement Award for the best new zoo exhibit in North America by the AZA in 2010.

The zoo continued to expand its role in breeding, rearing, and reintroducing endangered Northwest species, including Western pond turtles and Oregon silverspot butterflies. For the first time, the zoo also contributed to the release of Oregon spotted frogs. Washington State had listed this frog species as endangered in 1997, and a special rearing facility had been

Slow But Steady Wins the Race to Survive

In 1990, Western pond turtles in Washington State were in big trouble. The zoo's curator of reptiles Frank Slavens, in cooperation with the Washington Department of Fish and Wildlife, launched a turtle "head start" program.

Western pond turtles had once ranged from the Puget Sound lowlands in Washington all the way to Baja California, but they had just about vanished from the Puget Sound range by the 1980s. They had been a commercial food source into the early 20th century, and they were also eaten by non-native bullfrogs. Habitat loss and disease had added to their problems.

The effort to save them began in 1991 with the release of 27 head-start turtles. By 2000, the estimated wild population of pond turtles in the state had doubled, and by 2015, the program had helped reverse the fate of this native turtle. More than 2,100 turtles have been head-started and released, boosting the wild population from 150 turtles at two sites to more than 1,000 turtles at six sites. It was and continues to be Washington State's longest-running species reintroduction. At some sites, wild hatchlings also are surviving. Because the turtles were still in trouble in 2015, the yearly spring turtle and egg roundups were slated to continue for the foreseeable future.

Each spring, volunteers live-trap endangered Western pond turtles in the field, fitting adult females with transmitters so they can be tracked to their nests later in the season. The nests are then covered with screen cages to protect the eggs from predators.

A few months later, the WDFW return to collect the eggs and any young turtles that have hatched, taking them to Woodland Park Zoo or Oregon Zoo. The eggs are incubated until they hatch. Then the baby turtles are taken care of until the age of 8 or 10 months, when they get too big to be eaten by bullfrogs.

The Western pond turtle (*Actinemys marmorata*) has been known as the Pacific pond turtle, Western mud turtle, Pacific mud turtle, Pacific terrapin, and Pacific freshwater turtle. The medium-sized turtle lives up to 50 years and spends most of its life in water—streams, ponds, and wetlands—but it is known to bask on logs and nest on land. Female turtles begin reproducing between the ages of 8 to 12 years old, digging shallow nests to lay a clutch of 2 to 13 eggs.

The turtles get some extra help from project leaders and volunteers who remove non-native bullfrog egg masses from protected sites. From 1990 to 2000, no two- or three-year-old turtles were ever seen in the wild, but after that, they began showing up. Dr. Jennifer Pramuk, the zoo's curator of herpetology since 2010, along with VP of Field Conservation Dr. Fred Koontz, helped the zoo develop scientifically rigorous conservation standards for the project, and the zoo received the 2016 North American Conservation Award from AZA for this 25+ year collaborative program with a species in our own region.

For decades, the zoo and its volunteers have given endangered wild Western pond turtles a helping hand every breeding season.

established at the zoo. In September 2009, 450 endangered frogs reared by Woodland Park Zoo leapt into the wild at Dailman Lake in Pierce County, Washington.

Financial pressure from the 2008 recession—the worst since the Great Depression—had resulted in a big downturn in both donations and earned revenue at the zoo. At the same time, expenses were increasing. The zoo had to cut annual expenses by at least $800,000.

Closing the Night Exhibit—originally called the Nocturnal House—would save about $300,000 in a year. Completed in 1974, the Night Exhibit was a comparatively old building and one of the highest consumers of energy on zoo grounds. In January 2010, the zoo announced that the Night Exhibit would close on March 1.

Several Night Exhibit animals remained at the zoo. A pair of two-toed sloths moved to the Adaptations Building. The Rodrigues fruit bats, tamanduas (small anteaters native to South America), and springhaas (small rodents native to southeastern Africa) also moved to the Adaptations Building. A three-banded armadillo from the Night Exhibit was used in education programs. Since these animals are not completely nocturnal, they would be able to thrive in environments that did not have a reverse light cycle like the Night Exhibit.

In 2010, alert and popular meerkats returned to the zoo after a 10-year absence.

Animals moving to other accredited zoos included an Australian gray-headed bat, African straw-colored bats, vampire bats, coendous (arboreal porcupines), douroucoulis (owl monkeys), blind cave fish, and galagos (bush babies). Pygmy lorises stayed at the zoo, housed in an off-exhibit area for breeding.

A $150,000 meerkat project designed by staff opened to the public on May 1, 2010, the same day that a new West Entrance to the zoo opened, replacing the existing North and West entrances and reducing wait times at admission gates. Meerkats had been absent from the zoo's collection since 2000, when a major section of the Adaptations Building was remodeled to accommodate the Komodo dragons. When meerkats returned, keepers provided daily feedings and weekend talks for visitors all summer long.

On May 24, 2010, the zoo's oldest resident—a 57-year-old hippo named Gertrude—was euthanized. She had arrived at the zoo in 1966 at the age of 13. Fourteen years later, Gertie was one of the original inhabitants of the African Savanna and one of the first hippos to swim in the hippo pool. She suffered from complications due to age-related osteoarthritis, was in pain, and had become lame. At the time of her death, Gertie tipped the scales at about 5,000 pounds—nearly as much as two minivans.

In 2010, a mystery was finally solved. Where was Bobo's skull? Although it had been 42 years since the legendary gorilla died, everyone at the zoo knew about him. Bobo's skull had been missing ever since his death in 1968. It was returned to the Burke Museum after it was discovered among the effects of a recently deceased professor. With the return of the skull, the story of Bobo became news once again. He was a vivid part of Seattle's cultural history. Amazing changes had taken place at the zoo since the little ape arrived there in 1953, sporting a jacket, T-shirt, trousers, and suspenders.

Dana Payne: One of "the most fortunate of humans"

Dana Payne, curator of reptiles, began his career as a Snake House volunteer at age 18 in 1974.

With the death of Dana Payne on March 20, 2010, the zoo lost one of its most admired staff members and a champion of reptiles and amphibians. In 1974, at the age of 18, Payne started working as a volunteer in the Snake House—the Tropical House, later named the Day Exhibit. He became a zookeeper in 1983, a senior keeper in 1997, and a collection manager in 2001, and was promoted to curator of reptiles in 2003. Payne was the zoo's de facto historian and also the editor of its internal newsletter for most of his years at the zoo.

His advice was often solicited by zoo planners, and he participated on the design teams for several exhibits. He was also the fearless snake expert that the Seattle Police Department would call to confiscate venomous snakes under illegal ownership and the one to answer middle-of-the-night calls to supply antivenom for snakebite victims—often in other cities and states. Payne served on the team that developed an online Antivenom Index database where zoos post their inventories of antivenom. The database is consulted by poison control centers and hospitals throughout the country for emergency antivenom to treat victims of venomous snakebites.

His passion for protecting wildlife took him to Panama, where he helped El Valle Amphibian Conservation Center develop an online animal records system, critical for a holistic animal-care program. For many years, Payne was the steward of the zoo's Western Pond Turtle Recovery Project, and he initiated the zoo's leadership role in restoring populations of the Oregon spotted frog. Payne summed up his passion for Woodland Park Zoo in an end note for local artist Catherine Eaton Skinner's book, *Unleashed*:

> *Those of us who have chosen a life with animals know we have chosen well. Having a conversation with a lion is a fine way to start one's day. For that matter, so is tossing tidbits to a toucan, or medicating a cobra. There's something there, in the lion's luminous eyes, in the gaudy splendor of the toucan, in the cobra's sibilant protests: it's magic. It's the stuff of fairy tales to interact with animals like these, even in a scientific setting, and in spite of repetitious, routine chores. You should envy us, for we are the most fortunate of humans—we take care of the animals at the zoo.* (Catherine Eaton Skinner, *Unleashed*, University of Washington Press, 2009)

Dana Payne also worked in the field to conserve species, and served as the zoo's de facto historian and as the region's primary resource for snake-bite emergencies.

CHAPTER TWENTY

THE END OF ELEPHANTS,
A DELICATE BALANCE,
A GLOBAL REACH

IN SEPTEMBER 2011, Woodland Park Zoo was working with partners on 37 field conservation programs in 50 countries. To connect visitors to these efforts, the zoo began its Quarters for Conservation program. A quarter from every zoo admission would go directly to the zoo's field conservation program. Visitors got a token and used it at entrance kiosks to choose one of six rotating programs they wanted to fund. Visitors learned about the zoo's conservation work and felt a part of it at each visit. It was both fun and educational.

"Enrichment feeding" was another example of how the zoo planned events to serve multiple roles. In 2007, the zoo launched a new Thanksgiving event. Raw turkey carcasses were fed to many carnivores. Omnivores and herbivores got other Thanksgiving foods while the public—always interested in seeing animals *do* things—watched. The Halloween Pumpkin Bash had been offered since the early 1980s, and Valentine's Day

LEFT: The arrival of Komodo dragons drew big crowds.

ABOVE: Kiosks and signage in the zoo helped connect visitors with conservation programs.

and Fourth of July feedings also made their way onto the zoo's regular calendar.

Zoos all across the country were doing the same thing. In an October 17, 2015, article explaining this American custom to its readers, the UK's *Guardian* newspaper quoted Woodland Park Zoo's public relations and communications senior manager Gigi Allianic, saying that the purpose of enrichment feedings was "to promote natural animal behavior and keep animals

A wolf enjoys a Thanksgiving feast, 2014.

mentally stimulated." But of course the events were also publicized to attract visitors and made for adorable photos. Twenty-first-century zoos were often combining roles—in this case providing fun and frolic for humans that was also based on serious science about enriching the lives of the animals.

Nowhere did this multi-role aspect of Woodland Park Zoo create more conflict than with its plans for exhibiting and breeding elephants. Conservation, animal welfare, education, and the charismatic nature of elephants were all part of the mix, and feelings ran high. In 2015, the zoo made the difficult decision to end its elephant program because there were only two remaining elephants and no viable options for adding to the herd, and found a new home for them at the Oklahoma City Zoo. Suits were filed in state and federal courts to prevent the animals from leaving, but they were eventually dismissed and the elephants were moved.

As 2015 came to a close, the zoo announced that it would be seeking public comment and suggestions about what to do with the elephant exhibit area in the coming year. And after the elephants' departure, there was excitement about a female baby gorilla—the first gorilla born at the zoo in eight years. It was a reminder that there would be many new animals at the zoo in years to come.

Staff Celine Pardo and Gigi Allianic with penguin chick.

The elephant controversy had raised questions about what zoos should or shouldn't be doing—questions that hadn't arisen in earlier decades. But what had never changed was the role of the zoo as a place where children's natural interest in animals could be encouraged.

On April 3, 2012, a young boy looking at Humboldt penguins alerted keeper Celine Pardo that he could see an abandoned egg on a cliff in the exhibit. Pardo immediately rescued the egg, took it indoors and away from a predatory crow or gull, and placed it under a pair of foster parents.

She returned to the exhibit to thank the little boy, but he was gone. Two days later, the chick hatched. Pardo wanted to invite him back and take him behind the scenes to meet the chick and help name it. The zoo asked the public if they knew who he was, describing him as seven or eight years old with curly blond hair, wearing a white T-shirt. He was also characterized as "extremely polite." The mystery boy was never found, but the zoo named the penguin in his honor, giving him the name Ramón, a Spanish name that means "protector."

On May 5, 2012, rare and endangered Visayan (vih-SIGH-uhn) warty pigs were unveiled at an exhibit based on jungles of the Philippines. Because of their spiky head tufts, the zoo offered free admission to anyone sporting a Mohawk haircut. For those who didn't already have one, nearby Rudy's Barbershop would provide one at no cost.

In the African Savanna, wild pigs called warthogs made their debut at the same time. They got their name from the large facial warts on each side of their tusks. The character Pumbaa in Disney's *The Lion King* had familiarized lots of children with warthogs. The first 500 children who came to see the two new species on opening day got a free piggy bank, and there was also a program called "Pigs, Warts and All" with keeper talks and educational Zoomazium events.

Warthog in the African Savanna, 2015.

Triplet snow leopards, designated as "conservation ambassadors," were born on May 2. Snow leopard scientists estimated that as few as 4,000 were left in the wild. The zoo participated in the AZA Species Survival Plan for snow leopards, aimed at keeping a genetically diverse and viable population in accredited zoos in North America. Thirty-four snow leopards had been born at the zoo. Sadly, one of the triplets, born with severe heart defects, was later euthanized, and eye surgery was performed on the other two because of a condition known as multiple ocular coloboma.

The Era of Elephants Comes to an End

· · · · · · ·

The effort to breed Chai in 2011 was part of the AZA Species Survival Plan for elephants. AZA zoos had a common goal of creating multigenerational herds that provided the social structure so important to elephant well-being. Breeding had become vital to the future of elephants in American zoos because by 2003 importing them had been outlawed. If zoos wanted to continue to exhibit elephants, they would have to breed them.

But some people didn't want zoos to exhibit elephants at all. Earlier that year, on May 27, the King County Superior Court had dismissed a lawsuit against the City of Seattle by animal-rights advocates who said city funds should not be used to support the zoo's elephant program.

In December 2012, the *Seattle Times* ran a front-page, two-part, in-depth story called "Glamour Beasts: The Dark Side of Elephant Captivity." The series painted a grim picture of life for elephants in zoos, and described formerly cold, sickly elephants from zoos in Alaska and Detroit who were now living happily in a vast, warm California sanctuary without being exhibited, or bred.

Woodland Park Zoo responded with a press release and op-eds telling the public that elephants in zoos were vital to saving the species in the wild, enabling veterinarians and scientists to learn more about how they reproduce, and that zoo elephants served as "conservation emissaries," motivating humans to save the species in the wild.

Bamboo assists in the groundbreaking for a new Elephant House exhibit, 1987.

In October 2013, a zoo elephant task force reported that the zoo's three elephants—Watoto, Bamboo, and Chai—were in good health. But it also said, "Significant improvements are needed to improve the social well-being and behavioral health" of the three elephants, including enlarging the facility, reducing choke points in the barn, and giving them more enrichment activities. The report said that all three elephants showed varying degrees of weaving, rocking, or other repetitive behavior, but that they considered these moderate and not indicative of stress.

Most of the task force wanted the zoo to continue to try to develop a multigenerational herd and operate an active breeding program. The zoo took these recommendations on board, saying they planned to build a herd of more Asian elephants and spend $1.5 to $3 million on improving the exhibit and supporting conservation. A minority on the task force wanted the three elephants to live out their lives at the zoo, without an effort to breed them or increase the number of animals.

A local animal-rights activist group said the zoo had handpicked the task force members and hadn't invited input from any of the 14 elephant experts it had suggested. "The elephants didn't stand a chance," the group's leader wrote in an email response to the report. The group wanted the zoo to move the elephants to an elephant sanctuary and stop breeding attempts, saying that Chai had undergone invasive, uncomfortable artificial-insemination procedures 112 times.

In 2014, to celebrate World Elephant Day, August 12, Watoto was given a paintbrush and "signed her name" on a giant pledge form to "help her cousins in the wild." Bamboo did the same. The zoo had joined the 96 Elephants Campaign, led by more than 150 zoos, aquariums, and partners to help save elephants and shut down the ivory trade.

Ten days later, arthritic, 45-year-old Watoto was unable to get up, and the decision was made to humanely euthanize the geriatric animal. The zoo asked the community to honor her by taking action to save her species. As is usual, the death was an emotional time for animal care staff. Some of them had worked with her for 30 years.

The herd was now down to two individuals, and staff were concerned about their welfare. If one were to pass away, there were no other near-term options for bringing in another elephant. Although the zoo owned a third Asian elephant, Sri, she had been sent to the Saint Louis Zoo on a permanent breeding loan in 2002. In November 2014, the Woodland Park Zoo Society Board changed course. It said it would phase out the elephant program, and in 2015, send Chai and Bamboo to the Oklahoma City Zoo, which already had five Asian elephants ranging in age from 2 months to 47 years, in a $13 million, 9.5-acre exhibit with 3.95 acres available for the elephants, along with two pools and a waterfall.

The zoo explained that it had rejected California's 2,300-acre Performing Animal Welfare Society (PAWS) sanctuary, noting that it had only two elephants, and they were isolated from each other because of a tuberculosis infection, which would deprive Chai and Bamboo of social interaction. Their position was supported by wildlife biologist Jane Goodall, who was originally in favor of the move to a sanctuary, but changed her mind after talking to Woodland Park Zoo's Dr. Nancy Hawkes.

The group of local animal-rights activists were furious. They said the Oklahoma City Zoo would subject the elephants to freezing temperatures and the elephants would not have enough room. They urged the City Council to insist that the zoo send the elephants to a sanctuary, but that attempt failed. An allied group went to King County Superior Court, asking for a preliminary injunction to put the move on hold.

On April 3, 2015, Judge Palmer Robinson ruled in favor of the zoo. The sanctuary proponents went to federal court, but U.S. District Judge John C. Coughenour denied their request for an injunction to block the transfer of the elephants.

On April 15, keepers helped Chai and Bamboo walk onto a specialized elephant transport vehicle to begin their journey to Oklahoma. When the trip was rerouted because of bad weather, giving the elephants a rest stop at the San Diego Zoo, the activists were back in court, but by May, Chai and Bamboo were in their new home in Oklahoma and integrating into their new family.

Over the decades, elephants had served as living symbols of the zoo. The public knew them by name and treasured them as community icons.

Later that year, Woodland Park Zoo transferred legal ownership of Chai and Bamboo to the Oklahoma City Zoo, and ownership of Sri to the Saint Louis Zoo, where she had been living. The controversy was one of the most painful chapters in the zoo's history. During the years it went on, many other zoos, including the Philadelphia Zoo, Detroit Zoo, and San Francisco Zoo, also voluntarily discontinued their elephant programs.

The fraught episode revealed just how strongly both zoo professionals and the public felt about elephants. They always had, ever since the penny drive to buy Wide Awake and the decisions to rescue Tusko and accept Chai as a gift. What had evolved over many decades was an awareness of the threat to elephants in their native habitat as well as a more sophisticated understanding of the social and emotional needs of elephants.

But meanwhile, scientists had been tracking snow leopards in the wild since 2008 in conjunction with the International Snow Leopard Trust (ISLT). The trust was one of Woodland Park Zoo's conservation partners, and had been founded there in the 1970s. A month after the snow leopard triplets were born, ISLT scientists from Sweden, Mongolia, and Australia had some exciting news.

They were the first people to locate and provide video documentation of snow leopard mothers and cubs in den sites in the wild. Traveling through steep and rocky mountain outcroppings in southern Mongolia's Gobi Desert, the team followed VHF signals transmitted by GPS collars and located the dens on June 21. They took hair samples and implanted microchips in two of the cubs while their mother was out hunting. What they would learn in the field, as well as knowledge about the species gleaned at the zoo, would continue the work of the trust to save the species.

The zoo was always working on new ways to finance its many activities and engage the public at the same time. In December 2012, it came up with a new

Enjoying the zoo in a new light—WildLights 2013.

event to build traffic for one of the slowest times of the year. WildLights was a hit, and became an annual holiday season tradition. Animated displays in two and three dimensions were created with more than half a million colorful LED lights woven into the zoo's extensive greenery. The displays depicted animals and exotic habitats. Visitors, including many children, strolled along the transformed pathways and in the North Meadow and experienced the zoo in a whole new way. WildLights included visits with nocturnal animals, and with Santa Claus and visiting reindeer, as well as nighttime carousel rides and snacks.

By 2010, with a very active and creative curatorial team, Woodland Park Zoo had become a leader in breeding and care for many rare species of mammals, birds, reptiles, and amphibians. In 2013, this work resulted in a bit of a mammal baby boom—four lions, four small-clawed otters, three jaguars, two sloth bears, a giraffe, porcupine, wallaroo, and wallaby. The jaguars were especially meaningful because the sire, "Junior," had been brought here in 2005 as part of an AZA conservation consortium to assist a small zoo in Bolivia that was housing animals who had been rescued from persecution by ranchers.

On the evening of March 11, 2015, Woodland Park Zoo mammal curator Martin Ramirez picked up a special delivery from the Little Rock, Arkansas, Zoo at Sea-Tac Airport—three brothers named Liem, Eko, and Olan, 1½-year-old Malayan tiger brothers, weighing in at around 200 pounds apiece. They went into the regular 30-day quarantine that lets new animals get to know keepers while their health is monitored. Fewer than 300 individuals of their subspecies remained in the wild.

The tiger trio made its debut on May 2, at the grand opening of the zoo's Banyan Wilds exhibit, designed by Studio Hanson|Roberts. It was the zoo's most ambitious new project in nearly 20 years.

Events such as WildLights raised money for the zoo and developed new ways to engage the community.

both an $83 million fundraising campaign and a new strategic plan had been completed. Bruce Bohmke, a 16-year employee of the zoo, became acting president and CEO while the search for a new director began. Jensen went on to serve as Distinguished Practitioner in Residence at the University of Washington.

Her tenure had been a period of spectacular change and growth. The zoo had completed the transition from being a part of city government to an entity managed by the nonprofit Woodland Park Zoo Society. Jensen had helped establish the zoo as a leading conservation organization and presided over the creation of education programs serving everyone from toddlers to adults. She left behind an organization with more

Their exhibit costars were another endangered species —sloth bears. The shaggy animals are known as vacuum cleaners of the jungle. Long, flexible lips, missing front teeth, and a hollowed palate make it possible for them to remove masses of termites from their nests like a high-powered vacuum.

The two-acre exhibit, funded by more than 1,250 individuals, families, foundations, and corporations, included an impressive artificial banyan tree, monolithic rock formations evoking southern India, and the opportunity for visitors to see the animals both on their own at close range and interacting with keepers during training and enrichment activities. As a crucial part of the project, the zoo pledged $1 million to tiger conservation in Malaysia. Phase one had been launched in 2013 with Asian small-clawed otters, a tropical aviary, and a children's nature play area.

Deborah Jensen presided at the festive event held to dedicate the exhibit. About a month later, on June 8, she announced her resignation, effective at the end of July, after 13 years. She said the timing was right, as

Bruce Bohmke with a spectacled owl, 2006. Bruce joined the staff in 1999, became COO in 2002, and served as acting CEO June 2015 - May 2016.

than 40,000 member families, a budget of $36 million a year, and a $12 million endowment.

In May 2016, Alejandro Grajal, an executive at the Chicago area's Brookfield Zoo, became the eighth leader of the zoo in its 117-year history. Trained as a marine biologist, with a Ph.D. in zoology, he brought a global background in field conservation to Woodland Park Zoo. Before his work in Chicago, he had served as executive director of international programs for the National Audubon Society and director of Latin American programs at the Wildlife Conservation Society in New York, and been part of conservation programs with the United States Agency for International Development, the Global Environment Fund, the World Bank, and the European Union.

He has published widely, including co-authoring the book *Climate Change Education: A Primer for Zoos and Aquariums.* A native of Venezuela, Grajal is also a wildlife artist. He had long admired Woodland Park Zoo's reputation as a leader and innovator, and he shared its commitment to make conservationists out of everybody. "We'll turn 1.3 million visitors a year into social innovators and partners in real-time

Since the beginning, Woodland Park Zoo has been the place where people and animals connect.

conservation," he said. "We'll grow people's capacity as agents of change." He believed that zoos had important work to do both fostering the deep, affective bond between people and animals, and caring for the planet.

The role of director was a far cry from the early days, when Gus Knudson had worked out of an unheated shed, operating on a shoestring budget and railing against stingy funding that made even feeding the animals a challenge.

Over the years, there had been some tough times—the Depression, when the zoo couldn't even make payroll, and the war years, when the zoo became a low priority. During the prosperous 1950s, the zoo had modernized, become more professional, and begun working with other zoos around the country.

In the sixties and seventies, a period of sweeping social change, the zoo seemed to reinvent itself. It began many years of creating naturalistic exhibits, pioneering zoo design that spawned imitators and earned the zoo global respect. The zoo grew and prospered, became more of a regional institution, made a huge change in governance, and spread its influence all over the globe through conservation partnerships aligned with its animal collection back in Seattle.

But despite all this change, the basic idea behind the zoo had always been there, starting with Guy Phinney establishing a place for city dwellers to enjoy nature in a managed setting. His rules for Phinney park had included "Any person picking flowers, moss or cutting or marring any tree, shrub, plant or building will be arrested," and "Any person molesting or teasing any bird or animal or disturbing any bird's nest will be arrested."

Later, in 1922, director Gus Knudson elaborated on Phinney's mission by stating that the five goals of the park were to: "exhibit animals under favorable conditions; to foster and encourage zoological research;

to increase public interest and public knowledge in wild animals and birds; to secure better protection of animal life by educational methods; to attract people from out of town to visit Seattle." (1922 Annual Report to Seattle's Board of Park Commissioners)

In 1963, acting director Frank Vincenzi wrote: "Although the primary goal should be to preserve wild animals in their own natural habitat, zoos must accept responsibility for saving species whose existences are precarious. It is hoped that every consideration will be given to continued expansion of our facilities as a means of saving our seemingly doomed wildlife from extinction and preserving for future generations the opportunity to view and study these animals." And later, Director van Oosten proposed a revolutionary new plan that included "buildings impossible for the public to see."

From its beginnings, the zoo was seen as a place to educate citizens about animals from all over the globe. It was sometimes seen as a refuge for animals in need of a safe haven. From very early on, it was perceived by its directors as a place to expand scientific knowledge and to support conservation. It took the public a while longer to catch up with these ideas, but when they did, they embraced them.

For more than a century, millions of people have come to Woodland Park Zoo to see the animals. In 2015 alone, there were more than 1.3 million visitors. As humans have taken on new ways of looking at the world, the zoo has changed the way it fills all of its basic roles, and it will certainly continue to do so.

But everything the zoo has done over the decades is based on one simple, immutable truth: Beginning in childhood, humans have a strong emotional and intellectual desire to connect with the other animals on the planet we share.

FOLLOWING PAGE: Baby Yola, 2016.

ACKNOWLEDGMENTS

Our thanks and gratitude to those whose contributions made this book possible:

Alaska Airlines

Linda and Tom Allen

Richard and Nancy Alvord

Sally Barns

Sharon Billeter

Lynn Claudon

Jon Coe

Deb Crespin

Robert and Molly Davidson

Sheila Wycoff Dickey and Charles Dickey

Hugh and Jane Ferguson Foundation

Jane Foster

Richard and Ginger Goldman

Joshua and Pamela Green

Becca Hanson

Jan Hendrickson

Bruce and Carol Hosford

C. David Hughbanks

Dan and Darlene Huntington

Deborah Jensen

Ronald Johnson

Paula and John Karlberg

Bill Lewis

David and Melinda Littrell

Chuck Maise

Jim and Cynthia Maxwell

Doug and Joyce McCallum

Charlie and Alex Morse

Sue Nicol

Phil and Sandy Nudelman

Vic and Mary Odermat

Lynn Ormsby

Alan and Inger Osberg

Christopher and Janet Powell

Jeannette Reynolds

Robert and Diane Shrewsbury

Dale Sperling

John Swanson

Ace Torre

Dave and Chris Towne

Janet and Doug True

Maggie Walker

Michael Waller

Jana and Lynn Wilkins

Walter Williams Estate

Woodland Park Zoo Society

APPENDICES
WOODLAND PARK ZOO AWARDS

Exhibitry

2015   Washington Aggregates & Concrete Association, Excellence in Concrete Construction Award *(Banyan Wilds)*

2011   U.S. Green Building Council, Gold Certification, LEED® (Leadership in Energy and Environmental Design) Green Building Rating System™ *(West Entrance)*

2010   Association of Zoos & Aquariums (AZA), Exhibit Achievement Award *(Humboldt Penguin Exhibit)*. Exhibit Achievement Award recognizes the best new zoo exhibit in North America

2009   Seattle Design Commission, Design Excellence Award *(Humboldt Penguin Exhibit)*

2007   AIA Washington, 2007 Civic Design Awards – Citation *(Zoomazium)*

2007   U.S. Green Building Council, Gold Certification, LEED® (Leadership in Energy and Environmental Design) Green Building Rating System™ *(Zoomazium)*

2007   Associated Builders and Contractors (ABC) of Western Washington, Excellence in Construction Award for Sustainable Certified Construction: Kirtley-Cole Associates, LLC *(Zoomazium)*

2007   ParentMap, Readers' and Editors' Picks: Best Indoor Play Area *(Zoomazium)*

2006   *Seattle* magazine, selected a Best of 2006 standout, super-star and tastemaker: Best Place to Take Kids on a Rainy Day *(Zoomazium)*

2006   TEA (formerly Themed Entertainment Association), Thea Award for Outstanding Achievement: Zoo Exhibit *(Zoomazium)*

2006   *Northwest Construction* magazine, Best of 2006 Washington, Best Green Project *(Zoomazium)*

2005   AZA, Significant Achievement Award *(Jaguar Cove)*

2004   Associated Builders and Contractors of Western Washington, Excellence in Construction Award for Specialty Construction *(Jaguar Cove)*

2003   *Northwest Construction* magazine, Award of Excellence *(Jaguar Cove)*

1997   AZA, Significant Achievement Award *(Trail of Vines)*

1995   AZA, Exhibit Achievement Award *(Northern Trail)*

1994   Seattle Design Commission, Award for Contextual Design *(Rain Forest Food Pavilion)*

1993   AZA, Exhibit Achievement Award *(Tropical Rain Forest)*

1990   AZA, Exhibit Achievement Award *(Elephant Forest)*

1990   Washington Aggregates & Concrete Association, Excellence in Concrete Construction Award *(Elephant Forest)*

1990   American Society of Landscape Architects, National Merit Award *(Elephant Forest)*

1989   Washington Association of Landscape Professionals, Environmental Recognition Award for Excellence in the Support and Development of Quality Landscape Projects

1989   American Institute of Architects, Seattle Chapter, Award of Merit *(Elephant Forest)*

1985   American Society of Landscape Architects, Washington State Chapter Merit Award *(Elephant Forest)*

1981   AZA, Exhibit Achievement Award *(African Savanna)*

1980   American Society of Landscape Architects, President's Award of Excellence in Landscape Architectural Design for New Exhibits and Public Spaces *(Gorilla Exhibit, Marsh and Swamp, Primate Islands, African Savanna)*

1978   American Society of Landscape Architects, Washington Chapter Honor Award *(Waterfowl and Asian Primates Exhibits)*

1977   American Society of Landscape Architects, Merit Award in Recreational Planning *(Long-range Plan)*

Conservation

2016   AZA, North American Conservation Award, Recovering Western Pond Turtles in Washington State: a 25-Year Team Effort (in partnership with Oregon Zoo)

2014   AZA, International Conservation Award (Top Honors), Tree Kangaroo Conservation Program in Papua New Guinea (with Columbus Zoo, Roger Williams Park Zoo, Saint Louis Zoo, Oregon Zoo, Cleveland Metroparks Zoo, Milwaukee County Zoological Gardens, Minnesota Zoological Garden, Zoo New England, Riverbanks Zoo, Sedgwick County Zoo, Santa Fe Community College Teaching Zoo, Gladys Porter Zoo, Brevard Zoo, San Diego Zoo, Smithsonian National Zoological Park)

2012   AZA, North American Conservation Award, Oregon Spotted Frog Reintroduction Project, in partnership with Oregon Zoo and Northwest Trek

2012   AZA, Significant Achievement Award, Oregon Silverspot Captive Rearing Program, in partnership with Oregon Zoo

2008   AZA, Significant Achievement Award, International Conservation, Tarangire Elephant Project, in partnership with Wildlife Conservation Society, Lincoln Park Zoo, Reid Park Zoo, Kansas City Zoo, Indianapolis Zoo, Roger Williams Park Zoo, Jacksonville Zoo and Gardens and Milwaukee County Zoo

2003   AZA, International Conservation Award, Rodrigues fruit bat (with Philadelphia Zoo, Oregon Zoo, Disney's Animal Kingdom, Roger Williams Park Zoo, Blank Park Zoo, John Ball Zoo, Riverbanks Zoo, Folsom Children's Zoo and Biodome de Montreal)

2001   AZA, International Conservation Award, Matschie's tree kangaroo (with Roger Williams Park Zoo, Calgary Zoological Society, Columbus Zoo and Aquarium, Gladys Porter Zoo, Kangaroo Conservation Center, Miami Metro Zoo, Milwaukee County Zoo, Oregon Zoo, Philadelphia Zoo, Pittsburgh Zoo and PPG Aquarium, Riverbanks Zoo and Garden, San Antonio Zoo, Santa Fe Community Teaching College and Zoological Society of San Diego)

1999   AZA, International Conservation Award, Jamaican iguana recovery (with Fort Worth Zoo, San Diego Zoo, Indianapolis Zoo, Audubon Institute, Sedgwick County Zoo, Tulsa Zoo, Toledo Zoo, Central Florida Zoo, Columbus Zoo, Gladys Porter Zoo and Milwaukee County Zoo)

1994   AZA, Significant Achievement Award, Matschie's tree kangaroo (with National Zoo)

1992   Washington Department of Fish and Wildlife, Certificate of Appreciation, Western pond turtle

1991   AZA, Edward H. Bean Award (highest award of AZA), long-term propagation of Solomon Island leaf frog

1989   American Federation of Aviculture, first captive breeding of gold-whiskered barbet

1985   AZA, Propagation Certificate, wallaroo

1985   AZA, Significant Achievement Award, propagation of gray-winged trumpeter

1984   American Federation of Aviculture, first captive breeding of gray-winged trumpeter

1982   AZA, Propagation Certificate, lion-tailed macaque

1981   AZA, First Captive Breeding Certificate, Brazilian tanager

1981   American Game Bird Breeders Certificate, first captive breeding of Hartlaub's duck

1981   American Federation of Aviculture, first captive breeding of Brazilian tanager

1980   AZA, First captive breeding of Dominican tree frog

1979   AZA, First Captive Breeding Certificate, Hartlaub's duck

1979   International Wild Waterfowl Association, Outstanding Avicultural Achievement Award for Hartlaub's duck

Education

2015   AZA, Significant Achievement Award, Volunteer Engagement

2011   AZA, Education Achievement Award, Ready, Set, Discover. Education Achievement Award recognizes the best education program in North America

2008   AZA, Significant Achievement Award, Cultural Interpreter Program

2004   Cascade Land Conservancy, The John Stanford Education Achievement Award, Wild Wise statewide outreach program

2004   Environmental Education Association of Washington, Award for Organizational Excellence

2001   AZA, Significant Achievement Award, Wild Wise statewide outreach program

1997   AZA, Significant Achievement Award, Forest Explorers outreach program

Environmental Sustainability

2011   AZA, Green Significant Achievement Award, Comprehensive Sustainability Program

Leslie, Victoria H.
Lewis, Bill L.
Libby, Cammi R.
Liddell, Robert M.
Liffick, Stephen M.
Lipsky, Scott
Littrell, David L.
Maio, Joseph R.
Mar, Nancy L.
Marieskind, Helen I.
Martin, Penny
Martinez, R. Eric
Mayers, Marc G.
McCurdy, Brooke K.
McGavick, Gaelynn
McGraw, James C.
McKinney, Rev. Samuel B.
McMillan, Leigh A.
Mehrer, June
Millar, Julia D.
Millegan, Michael H.
Miller, Landon C.G.
Moe, Ann M.
Morse, Charles H.
Murphy, Kathryn
Nelson, Jane R.
North, Donald K.
Norwalk, Thomas H.
Nudelman, Phil
Odermat, Mary F.
Ogilvie, Kelly M.
Oppenheimer, John F.
Ormsby, Robert D.
Ostranger, Karen A.
Palmer, Edward P.
Parrish, Valerie
Passage, R. James
Pellegrino, Nancy D.
Perlin, Mary Pembroke
Peterson, Laura J.
Peterson, Louis D.
Phillips, Lawrence R.
Pigott, Virginia L.

Poll, Rosalind B.
Rademaker, Mary B.
Ragen, Cameron B.
Reichman, Thomas L.
Reis, Mark M.
Rhodes, Emery W.
Rind, Sherry A.
Roe, Jeffrey E.
Rosauer, Matt
Rosen, Leslie B.
Ross, Missy
Ryan, Jill A.
Ryder, Anne
Savoy, Patti S.
Scanlan, Kathy L.
Schofield, Kevin M.
Schumacher, Edward C.
Schwartz, Greg M.
Sexton, Rick W.
Short, Rob
Shoup, Allen C.
Shrewsbury, Diane M.
Sicktich, Elizabeth A.
Siegle, Ron C.
Sim, Sophorn
Simon, Jeff H.
Sleeper, Barbara L.
Slinker, Bryan K.
Sorensen, Gretchen A.
Spencer, Merrill P.
Sperling, Dale R.
Spurr, Joy M.
Stafford, William B.
Stanley, Ronald W.
Steers, Lucy B.
Stewart, Laurie L.
Svidran, Jacquie M.
Swanson, Richard S.
Taylor, Penny L.
Tejera, R. Jay
Terrell, W. Glenn
Thomas, Edward D.
Thompson, Tim

Tilden, Ronald L.
Tomlinson, Timothy T.
Towne, David L.
True, Douglas L.
True, Janet D.
True, Stephanie A.
Urick, Bill
Vance, Cyrus R.
Vange, Darrell M.
Vladimer, Andres
Walker, Jill L.
Walker, Linda R.
Walker, Maggie
Wall, Irene M.
Wang, Peter C.
Wappler, Andrew
Weed, Julie C.
Werlinger, Heike
Wetherald, Margaret E.
Williams, Kathryn A.
Williams, Robert M.
Williams, Stuart V.
Winters, Dicksy
Wolff, Ben
Wright, Sally S.
Wyckoff, Susan S.
Wyckoff-Dickey, Sheila A.
Young, Curtis H.

Ex-Officio Board Members

Aguirre, Jesús
Bergeson, Terry
Bigelow, John C.
Bohmke, Bruce W.
Bolling, Wayne L.
Bounds, Kenneth R.
Brooks, Betty Jean
Campbell, Lori
Cole, Norma J.
Dahlgren, Amie M.
Davidson, Robert W.
Davis, Peter H.

Dvornich, Karen M.
Eberhardt, Dayna
Freeman, Helen E.
Gallagher, Timothy
Gibbs, Ron I.
Gibson, Lori I.
Grajal, Alejandro
Hagge, Deborah K.
Hancocks, David N.
Hawkins, Jerome L.
Hill, Kevin M.
Hogue, Mary H.
Holmes, Rob
Jensen, Deborah B.
Johnson, Gene
Klein, Judy D.
Lekisch, Jennifer
Martin, Stacy A.
Meredith, Carol E.
Merry, Carol J.
Meyers, Kenneth J.
Miller, Holly
Miller, Jean K.
Newton, Shelby E.
Olchefske, Joseph
Parker, Emily L.
Ping, Marilyn L.
Pritchard, Frank A.
Quirk, Linda J.
Roberts, Michael
Rose, Penny L.
Runyon, Katherine L.
Scanlan, Kathy L.
Segesta, Mary
Swanson, Richard S.
Towne, David L.
Treff, Nicole
Uhlman, Wes
Waller, Michael A.
Weed, Julie C.
Weltzin, Janis L.
Williams, Christopher

Williams, Walter B.
Wuersten, Eric
Zehnder, Amanda

Zoo Commission I 1984-85

Anderson, Virginia
Betrozoff, John W.
Blyth, Linda
Borah, William
Coffey, Forrest G. "Bud"
Cronin, William F.
Davidson, Robert W.
Jensen, Claus
Johnson, B. Gerald
Johnson, James
Jones, Beverly
Kilburn, Kumi
Kurtz, T. Russell, D.V.M.
Livesey, Deborah
Meadows, Robert G.
Murphy, Susan
Nagel, Joe
North, Donald K.
North, Lois
Nudelman, Phil
Pomarantz, Linda B.
Pritchard, Frank
Purnell, Carolyn
Raleigh, William H., D.D.S.
Riggs, Phyllis
Rodgers, Elizabeth
Smith, Chris
St. Louis, Mary Ann
Steers, Lucy
Sullivan, William J., S.J.
Swanson, Richard S.
Thomson, Terry E.
Van Ness, Virginia
Williams, Walter B., Chair
Yanick, Barbara T.

Zoo Commission II 1995

Arntz, William
Benaroya, Donna
Blackbourn, Jahn
Bunting, Kenneth
Crowley, Walt
Duff, George
Enticknap, Joan
Hattori, Jim
Huntington, Daniel
Ikeda, Gary
Johnson, Gerry
Jones, Jan
Judd, Ron
Kellogg, Matt
Kelly, Duane
Kushlan, Phil
Lazarus, Patty
Lewis, Bill
Lindsey, David
Madenwald, Darlene
Masterjohn, John
McGhie, Austin
McReynolds, Neil
Mitchell, Charles
Morefield, John
Morris, Steven
Nielsen, Don
Nudelman, Phil, Chair
Orlans, Gordon
Ormsby, Bob
Pitts, Sharon
Ratliffe, Robert
Reich, Jay
Rolls, Sam
Ryan, Jill
Swanson, Dick
Vange, Darrell
Wall, Irene
Wright, Vim C.

BIBLIOGRAPHY

Aweeka, Charles, and Val Varney. "Van Oosten 'one angry man' not quitting zoo battle." *Seattle Times*, September 22, 1974.

Bagley, Clarence. *History of King County, Washington*. Chicago & Seattle: S. J. Clarke Publishing Company, 1929.

Bartholick, George. *Comprehensive Plan Study*, Interim Report No. 1, 1970.

Bartholick, George. *Comprehensive Plan for Woodland Park Zoo*, 1972.

Berens, Michael. "Glamour Beasts: The Dark Side of Elephant Captivity." *Seattle Times*, December 2, 2012.

Beston, Henry. *The Outermost House*. Garden City, NY: Doubleday, Doran and Company, 1928.

Chozick, Amy. "The Leopards' New Spot." *Wall Street Journal*, June 12, 2009.

Coe, Jon. "Design and Perception: Making the Zoo Experience Real." *Zoo Biology*, 4 (2), 1985.

Coe, Jon. "Designing with People." *AZA Communiqué*, July 1997.

Coe, Jon. "Towards a Co evolution of Zoos, Aquariums and Natural History Museums." Annual Conference Proceedings of the American Association of Zoological Parks and Aquariums, 1986.

Coe, Jon. "What's the Message? Education Through Exhibit Design." In *Wild Mammals in Captivity: Principles and Techniques*, 167-174. Chicago: University of Chicago Press, 1997.

Crockett, Carolyn, and Michael Hutchins, editors. *Applied Behavioral Research at the Woodland Park Zoological Gardens*. Seattle: Pika Press, 1978.

Crowley, Walt. *The Woodland Park Zoo Guide*. Woodland Park Zoological Society, 1995

Final Report of the Citizen's Advisory Committee for the Seattle Zoo, July 1971.

Fryer, Alex. "Former Zoo Director Jan van Oosten, 71, Dies." *Seattle Times*, May 7, 2005.

Grazian, David. *American Zoo: A Sociological Safari*. Princeton, NJ: Princeton University Press, 2015.

Hancocks, David. *Animal Kingdom* insert, December 1982/January 1983.

Hancocks, David. *Animals and Architecture*. New York: Praeger, 1971.

Hancocks, David. *A Different Nature: The Paradoxical World of Zoos and Their Uncertain Future*. Berkeley: University of California Press, 2001.

Hancocks, David. "Former Woodland Park Head Sees Sad Future for Elephants in OK." Crosscut.com, April 2, 2015.

Hancocks, David. *Master Builders of the Animal World*. New York: Harper & Row, 1973.

Hediger, Heini. *Studies of the Psychology and Behaviour of Captive Animals in Zoos and Circuses*. London: Butterworth, 1955.

Herberg, Ruth. "Guy Phinney, Horatio Alger's Kind of Man." *North Seattle Press*, 1986.

The Inside Scoop, May 2004, Volume I (Woodland Park Zoo in-house publication).

Jones, Grant. "Beyond Landscape Immersion." In the Annual Conference Proceedings of the American Association of Zoological Parks and Aquariums, 1989.

Jones, Grant, with Jon Coe and Dennis Paulson. *Woodland Park Zoo: Long-Range Plan, Development Guidelines and Exhibit Scenarios*. Jones & Jones for Seattle Department of Parks and Recreation, 1976.

Linden, Eugene. *The Parrot's Lament: And Other True Tales of Animal Intrigue, Intelligence, and Ingenuity*. New York: Dutton, 1999.

McHarg, Ian. *Design with Nature*. Garden City, NY: Natural History Press for the American Museum of Natural History, 1969.

Nance, Susan. *Entertaining Elephants: Animal Agency and the Business of the American Circus*. Baltimore: Johns Hopkins University Press, 2013.

Olmsted Report on Woodland Park, 1903.

Paynter, Susan. "Woodland Park Zoo Staff Is Feeling Fenced In." *Seattle Post-Intelligencer*, August 19, 2007.

Pedersen, Ted. *Images of America: Seattle's Greenwood-Phinney Neighborhood*. Charleston, SC: Arcadia Publishing, 2008.

Plant Guide: Woodland Park Zoological Gardens. Washington Park Arboretum Bulletin, Volume 58.3.

Reynolds, Jeannette Johnson. Three personal scrapbooks.

Sherwood, Don. *Sherwood Park History Files*. Seattle Parks and Recreation, Municipal Archives.

Valdes, Manuel. "Guide and Zoo President Defend Maasai Role." *Seattle Times*, August 9, 2007.

Van Oosten, Jan. "The Zoo Changes Its Spots." *Puget Soundings*, December 1972. Published by the Junior League of Seattle, Inc.

Woodland Park Zoo Annual Reports to Seattle's Board of Park Commissioners, 1904-2009.

Woodland Park Zoo Commission Report, 1985.

Woodland Park Zoo press releases, miscellaneous.

"The Zoo: Loving Touch." *Time* magazine, June 23, 1967.

PHOTO CREDITS

All images courtesy of Woodland Park Zoo photo archive except where indicated:

1:	Dennis Dow
2:	Dennis Dow
3:	Ryan Hawk
5:	Jeremy Dwyer-Lindgren
8:	Zoo Society, Susan Okazaki
12a:	University of Washington Libraries, Special Collections, UW4996
12b:	Courtesy Jeannette Reynolds
13:	Courtesy of the Seattle Municipal Archives
14a:	University of Washington Libraries, Special Collections, UW37721
14b:	Courtesy of the Seattle Municipal Archives
16:	Museum of History and Industry, 2002.3.1817
17:	Museum of History and Industry, 1980.6967.15
18:	University of Washington Libraries, Special Collections, UW49920
19:	Courtesy of the Seattle Municipal Archives
23:	WPZ, Courtesy Gayle Knudson
24:	Courtesy of the Seattle Municipal Archives
29b:	WPZ, Courtesy Gayle Knudson
32:	Courtesy of the Seattle Municipal Archives
33:	Courtesy of the Seattle Municipal Archives
38:	Courtesy Jeannette Reynolds
39:	Courtesy Jeannette Reynolds
41:	Courtesy Jeannette Reynolds
43-45a:	Courtesy Jeannette Reynolds
45b:	Courtesy the Berry Family
47:	Courtesy Jeannette Reynolds
49a:	Courtesy of the Seattle Municipal Archives
55:	Museum of History and Industry, P124760
59:	MOHAI, *Seattle Post-Intelligencer* Collection, 1986.5.10390
62:	Dennis Dow
64a-b:	Courtesy of the Seattle Municipal Archives
72a:	Museum of History and Industry, 2000.107_print_ VanOosten, Jan

73:	The van Oosten Family
74a:	Museum of History and Industry, 2000.107.014.14.38
74b-75a:	Courtesy of the Seattle Municipal Archives
75b-76:	Dennis Dow
80-81:	Ryan Hawk
84:	Jeremy Dwyer-Lindgren
91:	Monika Fiby
92:	Dennis Dow
93:	Museum of History and Industry, 2000.107_print_ VanOosten, Jan
98:	Ryan Hawk
102a:	Jeremy Dwyer-Lindgren
103:	Ryan Hawk
104:	Dennis Dow
108:	Dennis Dow
109:	Sue Maloney Nicol Collection
110b:	Ryan Hawk
111:	Museum of History and Industry, 2000.107.086.34.01
113:	Courtesy Dave and Chris Towne
114:	Jeremy Dwyer-Lindgren
115:	Zoo Society, Susan Okazaki
116:	Dennis Dow
117:	Museum of History and Industry, 2000.107.179.17.01
118:	Museum of History and Industry, 2000.107.179.06.03
119b:	Museum of History and Industry, 2000.107.179.15.01
120b:	Museum of History and Industry, 2000.107.179.06.02
121:	Museum of History and Industry, 2000.107.179.06.01
122:	Ryan Hawk
124:	Dennis Dow
127b:	Ryan Hawk
128a:	Dennis Dow
128b:	Courtesy Jeannette Reynolds
128c:	Dennis Dow
130:	Dennis Dow
131:	Ryan Hawk
132:	Jeremy Dwyer-Lindgren
134a-b:	Ryan Hawk
135:	Dennis Dow
136b-137a:	Dennis Dow
138:	Mat Hayward
140-144b:	Dennis Dow
145:	Ryan Hawk

147:	Mike Waller
148:	Ryan Hawk
149:	Courtesy Jeannette Reynolds
150:	Dennis Dow
151:	Matt Hagen
152a:	Mat Hayward
152b-153a:	Dennis Dow
153b-154:	Ryan Hawk
155a-b:	Dennis Dow
158:	Jeremy Dwyer-Lindgren
160a:	Ryan Hawk
160b:	Dennis Dow
161a:	Ryan Hawk
161b:	Courtesy Peter Blecha
162-164:	Ryan Hawk
165:	Dennis Dow
166:	Mat Hayward
168a:	Dennis Dow
168b:	Ryan Hawk
169a:	Dennis Dow
170-171:	Ryan Hawk
172:	Dennis Dow
173b:	Ryan Hawk
174:	Dennis Dow
175a-b:	Ryan Hawk
176a:	Dennis Dow
176b:	Ryan Hawk
177:	Dennis Dow
179:	Ryan Hawk
180:	Jeremy Dwyer-Lindgren
181a:	Ryan Hawk
182:	Ryan Hawk
184:	Jeremy Dwyer-Lindgren
200:	Chris Towne

INDEX

Page numbers in *italics* indicate photographs.

Watercolor by Chris Towne: *Flock of Flamingos at Woodland Park Zoo.*